ENGLISH

FOR BUSINESS MEETINGS

Dhirawit Pinyonatthagarn

Ph.D. (Linguistics)

ENGLISH FOR BUSINESS MEETINGS

1. Course Overview & Objectives

The main purpose of this course is to help non-native English speakers develop essential meeting management competence and related skills in an English-speaking business environment. English will therefore be used at the primary teaching tool and communication mode. The course will enable participants to answer questions such as:

- What is necessary to have a productive meeting?
- How can I become an effective chairperson and participant?
- How can I manage people in order to meet stated goals?
- How can I use questions to facilitate the meeting presentation process?

By the end of the course, students should have been able to:

- Understand the various types of meetings and how they impact the results of meetings
- Manage any circumstances that may arise
- Improve their ability to meet objectives in a time efficient manner
- Feel more comfortable and confident as a chairperson and participant
- Better manage the overall meeting process including the handling of questions

2. Course Outline

Unit 1: Basic Words, Phrases, and Sentences

Unit 2: Introduction to Business Meetings

Unit 3: Business Meetings in Action

Unit 4: How to Conduct Business Meetings

Unit 5: Teleconference & Videoconference

Unit 6: Brainstorming

3. Grading Criteria

1. Class Attendance 5%
2. ELRU/Ellis Package 5%
3. Class Assignments/Projects 40%
4. Final 60%

4. Class Activities:

Lectures/Discussions/RolePlays/Tapes/MP//VDO/DVD

Contents

UNIT 1

BASIC WORDS, PHRASES, AND SENTENCES

OBJECTIVES

Upon the completion of this unit, students should have been able to:

1) get acquainted with useful words, phrases, sentences, and proper language use for business meetings
2) understand basic meeting words, phrases, and sentences
3) use those words, phrases, and sentences for the meeting purposes
4) understand functional language for performing well in the meeting

Task 1: Warm-up activity.

Instructions: Study these top 20 words in business meetings in column A and match them with their meaning in column B by putting the correct letter in front of the words from 1-20.

	A	B
_____ 1	A.G.M.	a) a type of vote, usually in writing and usually secret-*secret ballot*
_____ 2	A.O.B.	b) the person who leads or presides at a meeting; chairperson; chair
_____ 3	absent	c) in complete agreement; united in opinion
_____ 4	agenda	d) item on agenda for discussion of what has happened as a result of last meeting
_____ 5	apologies	e) to express opinion in a group by voice or hand etc - *also n.* - to cast a vote *v.*
_____ 6	ballot	f) item on agenda announcing people who are absent; apologies for absence
_____ 7	casting vote	g) a written record of everything said at a meeting
_____ 8	chairman	h) telephone call between three or more people in different locations
_____ 9	conference	i) general agreement

	A	**B**
_____10	conference call	j) a separate point for discussion [as listed on an agenda]
_____11	consensus	k) raised hands to express an opinion in a vote
_____12	decision	l) a deciding vote (usually by the chairman) when the votes are otherwise equal
_____13	item	m) Any Other Business [usually the last item on an agenda]
_____14	matters arising	n) a vote cast by one person for or in place of another
_____15	minutes	o) a written program or schedule for a meeting
_____16	proxy vote	p) formal meeting for discussion, esp. a regular one held by an organization
_____17	show of hands	q) a conclusion or resolution to do something to decide v.
_____18	unanimous	r) not here; not at the meeting; not present
_____19	videoconference	s) formal meeting for discussion, esp. a regular one held by an organization
_____20	vote	t) Annual General Meeting

(Adapted from: *Top Twenty Business Vocabulary*. www.englishclub.com/business-english/meetings.htm)

Task 2: Useful phrases and sentences

Instructions: Study and practice these phrases and sentences, individually, in pairs, or in groups.

A. FROM BEGINNING TO THE END

1. Opening the meeting
a) Good morning/afternoon, everyone.
b) If we are all here, let's get started/start the meeting/start.

2 Welcoming and introducing participants
a) Please join me in welcoming (name of participant)
b) We're pleased to welcome (name of participant)
c) It's a pleasure to welcome (name of participant)
d) I'd like to introduce (name of participant)
e) I don't think you've met (name of participant)

3. Stating the principal objectives of a meeting
a) We're here today to
b) Our aim is to ...
c) I've called this meeting in order to ...
d) By the end of this meeting, I'd like to have ...

4. Giving apologies for someone who is absent
a) I'm afraid.., (name of participant) can't be with us today.
b) She is in...
c) I have received apologies for the absence of (name of participant), who is in (place).

5. Reading the minutes (notes) of the last meeting

a) First let's go over the report from the last meeting, which was held on (date)

b) Here are the minutes from our last meeting, which was on (date)

6. Dealing with recent developments

a) Jandara, can you tell us how the XYZ project is progressing?

b) Jenjira, how is the XYZ project coming along?

c) Jampa, have you completed the report on the new accounting package?

d) Has everyone received a copy of the Siam Foundation report on current marketing trends?

7. Moving forward

a) So, if there is nothing else we need to discuss, let's move on to today's agenda.

b) Shall we get down to business?

c) Is there any other business?

d) If there are no further developments, I'd like to move on to today's topic.

8. Introducing the agenda

a) Have you all received a copy of the agenda?

b) There are three items on the agenda. First,

c) Shall we take the points in this order?

d) If you don't mind, I'd like to ... go in order

e) skip item 1 and move on to item 3

f) I suggest we take item 2 last.

9. Allocating roles (secretary, participants)
a) (name of participant) has agreed to take the minutes.
b) (name of participant) has kindly agreed to give us a report on this matter.
c) (name of participant) will lead point 1, (name of participant) point 2, and (name of participant) point 3.
d) (name of participant), would you mind taking notes today?

10. Agreeing on the ground rules for the meeting (contributions, timing, decision-making, etc.)
a) We will hear a short report on each point first, followed by a discussion round the table.
b) I suggest we go round the table first.
c) The meeting is due to finish at...
d) We'll have to keep each item to ten minutes. Otherwise we'll never get through.
e) We may need to vote on item 5, if we can't get a unanimous decision.

11. Introducing the first item on the agenda
a) So, let's start with
b) Shall we start with. .
c) So, the first item on the agenda is
d) Pairot, would you like to kick off?
e) Martin, would you like to introduce this item?

12. Closing an item
a) I think that covers the first item.
b) Shall we leave that item?
c) If nobody has anything else to add,

13. Next item
a) Let's move onto the next item
b) The next item on the agenda is
c) Now we come to the question of.

14. Giving control to the next participant
a) I'd like to hand over to Mark, who is going to lead the next point.
b) Right, Duangdao, over to you.

15. Summarizing
a) Before we close, let me just summarize the main points.
b) To sum up, ...
c) In brief,
d) Shall I go over the main points?

16. Finishing up
a) Right, it looks as though we've covered the main items
b) Is there Any Other Business?

17. Suggesting and agreeing on time, date and place for the next meeting
a) Can we fix the next meeting, please?
b) So, the next meeting will be on... (day), the . . . (date) of.. . (month) at...
c) What about the following Wednesday? How is that?
d) So, see you all then.

18. Thanking participants for attending
a) I'd like to thank Marianne and Jeremy for coming over from London.
b) Thank you all for attending.
c) Thanks for your participation.

19. Closing the meeting
a) The meeting is closed.
b) I declare the meeting closed.

B. DURING THE MEETING

1) Interrupting
a) May I have a word?
b) If I may, I think...
c) Excuse me for interrupting.
d) May I come in here?

2) Giving opinions
a) I (really) feel that...
b) In my opinion...
c) The way I see things...
d) If you ask me,... I tend to think that...

3) Asking for opinions
a) Do you (really) think that...
b) (name of participant) can we get your input?
c) How do you feel about...?

4) Commenting on other opinions
a) I never thought about it that way before.
b) Good point!
c) I get your point.
d) I see what you mean.

5) Agreeing with other opinions
a) Exactly!
b) That's (exactly) the way I feel.
c) I have to agree with (name of participant).

6) Disagreeing with other opinions
a) Up to a point I agree with you, but...
b) (I'm afraid) I can't agree

7) Advising and suggesting
a) We should...
b) Why don't you....
c) How/What about...
d) I suggest/recommend that...

8) Clarifying
a) Have I made that clear?
b) Do you see what I'm getting at?
c) Let me put this another way...
d) I'd just like to repeat that...

9) Requesting information
a) I'd like you to...
b) Would you mind... I wonder if you could...

10) Asking for repetition
a) I didn't catch that. Could you repeat that, please?
b) I missed that. Could you say it again, please?
c) Could you run that by me one more time?

11) Asking for clarification
a) I'm afraid I don't quite understand what your are getting at.
b) Could you explain to me how that is going to work?
c) I don't see what you mean. Could we have some more details, please?

12) Asking for verification
a) Do you mean that...?
b) Is it true that...?

13) Asking for spelling
a) Would you mind spelling that for me, please?
b) How do you spell that?
c) What's the spelling of that?

14) Asking for contributions for other participants
a) What do you think about this proposal?
b) Would you like to add anything, (name of participant)?
c) Has anyone else got anything to contribute?
d) Are there any more comments?

15) Correcting information
a) Sorry, that's not quite right.
b) I'm afraid you don't understand what I'm saying.
c) That's not quite what I had in mind.
d) That's not what I meant.

16) Keeping the meeting on time
a) Well, that seems to be all the time we have today.
b) Please be brief.
c) I'm afraid we've run out of time.
d) I'm afraid that's outside the scope of this meeting.
e) Let's get back on track, why don't we?
f) That's not really why we're here today.
g) Why don't we return to the main focus of today's meeting.
h) We'll have to leave that to another time.
i) We're beginning to lose sight of the main point.
j) Keep to the point, please.
k) I think we'd better leave that for another meeting.
l) Are we ready to make a decision?

(Adapted from: www.scribd.com/doc/2740308/English-for-business-meeting)

Task 3
Questions A
Instructions: Choose the best answer (a, b, c, or d) for the following questions.

1. Which one is NOT an expression for opening the meeting?
   - a) Good morning
   - b) Good afternoon
   - c) Good evening
   - d) Good night

2. Which one is an expression for welcoming participants?
   - a) I'd like to introduce...
   - b) Please join me in welcoming...
   - c) If we are all here, let's get started.
   - d) I don't think you have met...

3. You can start the principal objectives of the meeting by saying...
   - a) We're here today to...
   - b) Our aim is to...
   - c) I've called this meeting in order to ...
   - d) All of these

4. What do you say when you want to move forward?
   - a) So, if there is nothing else we need to discuss, let's move on to today's agenda.
   - b) Shall we get down to business?
   - c) If there are no further developments, I'd like to move on to today's topic.
   - d) a and c are correct

5. Which is NOT an expression for introducing the agenda?
      a) Have you all received a copy of the agenda?
      b) There are three items on the agenda. First,...
      c) Shall we take the points in this order?
      d) Would you mind taking notes today?

6. How do you introduce the first item on the agenda?
      a) Shall we start with...?
      b) So, the first item on the agenda is...
      c) Pete, would you like to kick off?
      d) All of these.

7. Which one is NOT an expression for moving onto the next item?
      a) Let's move onto the next item.
      b) The next item on the agenda is...
      c) Now we come to the question of...
      d) That's not true.

8. What do you say to summarize the meeting?
      a) Before we close, let me just summarize the main points.
      b) To sum up, ...
      c) Shall I go over the main points?
      d) All of these

9. Which one is an expression for suggesting and agreeing on time, date and place for the next meeting?
      a) Can we fix the next meeting, please?
      b) So, the next meeting will be on... (day), the . . . (date) of.. . (month) at...
      c) What about the following Wednesday? How is that?
      d) All of these

10. What do you say to close the meeting?
  a) The meeting is closed.
  b) I declare the meeting closed.
  c) Can I close the meeting?
  d) a and b are correct

11. Which one is an expression for interrupting?
  a) May I have a word?
  b) I don't think so.
  c) That's great.
  d) I like that.

12. What do you say to give opinions?
  a) I (really) feel that...
  b) In my opinion,...
  c) The way I see things,...
  d) All of these

13. How do you ask for opinions?
  a) Do you (really) think that...?
  b) Can we get your input?
  c) How do you feel about...?
  d) All of these.

14. Which is an expression for agreeing with other opinions?
  a) Exactly!
  b) That's (exactly) the way I feel.
  c) I am sorry.
  d) a and b

15. What do you say to disagree with other opinions?
  a) I agree with you, but...
  b) (I'm afraid) I can't agree.
  c) a and b
  d) None of these

16. Which one is NOT an expression for advising and suggesting?
   a) We should...
   b) Why don't you....
   c) I suggest/recommend that...
   d) I wish I could.

17. What do you say when you want to clarify things?
   a) Have I made that clear?
   b) Do you see what I'm getting at?
   c) Let me put this another way...
   d) All of these

18. Which is an expression to ask for repetition?
   a) I didn't mean that.
   b) I missed that. Could you say it again, please?
   c) Could you come again tomorrow?
   d) What's it like?

19. How do you ask for contributions from other participants?
   a) What do you think about this proposal?
   b) Would you like to add anything,
      (name of participant)?
   c) Has anyone else got anything to contribute?
   d) All of these.

20. Which one is NOT an expression for keeping the meeting on time?
   a) Well, that seems to be all the time we have today.
   b) I'm afraid we've run out of time.
   c) Absolutely!
   d) Keep to the point, please.

Task 3
Questions B
Instructions: Match the language in Column B with their function in Column A.

Meetings – Language

A. Function	B. Language
1. Starting	A. Many thanks for coming, shall we start?
2. Disagreeing	B. We need to discuss..
3. Agreeing	C. What do you think about..?
4. Asking for an opinion	D. I agree. I totally agree!
5. Introducing the subject	E. I don't agree
6. Partially conceding	F. Yes, you are right there.
7. Conceding a point	G. I can see your point but...
8. Making an opinion	I. I think we should...
9. Suggesting an alternative	G. Why don't we...instead?
10. Making a proposal	K. In my opinion.
11. Presenting alternatives	L. Would you mind giving us your views on this?
12. Asking for participation	M. We can either ... or ...
13. Bringing back the focus of the discussion	N. We are drifting away from the subject. Can we concentrate on the main points?
14. Ending	O. Many thanks for your participation. It's been a productive meeting.

UNIT 2

INTRODUCTION TO BUSINESS MEETINGS

OBJECTIVES

Upon the completion of this unit, students should have been able to:

1) Understand the nature of business meetings
2) Know how to prepare for the meeting
3) Participate effectively in the meeting
4) Plan the meeting
5) Chair the meeting
6) Run the meeting efficiently

Task 1: Warm-up activity.

Instructions: Look up in the dictionary and write out the meanings of the following words.

1. pet
   peeve(n.)_____

   _____

2. unavoidable(adj.)_____

   _____

3. dynamic(adj.)_____

   _____

4. inspirational(adj.)_____

   _____

5. destination(n.)_____

   _____

6. facilitator(n.)_____

   _____

7. competent(adj.)_____

   _____

8. appropriate(adj.)_____

_____

9. determine(v.)_____

_____

10. strategy(n.)_____

_____

Task 2: Gap filling

Instructions: Read the following passages about English business meeting and fill in the blanks with the words provided below.

brought involve agenda present language conference standpoint formal meetings business

Business meetings conducted in English are either _____ or informal. The informal variety may involve only a couple of people and take place in the managers, or your own, office. For this type there may not be a set time or agenda. Formal meetings usually _____ larger numbers of people and are often held in a conference room. There will be an agenda and minutes (detailed notes) are taken to record what happened in the meeting

An _____ lists out the time and place of the meeting and also the points that will have to be covered. Quite often there is also a section of time allocated to "Any other business" (AOB) where ideas that are not listed on the agenda may be _____ up for discussion.

Formal _____ may involve a presentation (sales presentation or otherwise) being given, and details on how to conduct effective presentations are covered elsewhere on this site. It is good to familiarize yourself with the venue, however, should you be asked to _____ something ad-hoc using the white board or flip chart.

As in all communication, body _____ is very important. Don't smile too much but again don't look totally bored. Holding a pencil in both hands shows that you are paying attention. Sitting at the corner of a _____ table can sometimes give you superiority.

The actual language used in English_____ meetings is detailed below but is not exclusive. Conceding or partially conceding is a good way to negotiate your point of view into being accepted whereas totally disagreeing, or raising your voice is likely to induce hostility and end up with your _____ being overturned.

(Adapted from: www.hkenglish.com/business-meetings.html)

Task 3: Reading comprehension

Instructions: Read the following passages and answer the questions that   follow.

a) The Nature of Meeting

My two pet peeves are being stuck in mismanaged meetings and in traffic jams. Traffic jams are often unavoidable but ineffective meetings are particularly irksome since it is simple to plan and manage successful meetings. Using the tools for creating dynamic and inspirational meetings doesn't require a Ph.D. or months of training. Why then are these simple ideas and tools so often ignored?

Meetings are too often seen as an end unto themselves. We've attended more than our share of meetings where the object was to get to the meeting. Once there, we dutifully filled the time allotted while producing only a minimum of new ideas,   plans   and   action.

Using   meetings   effectively   starts   with   the understanding   that   **meetings   are   not   the destination but a vehicle** for reaching strategic objectives or organizational destinations. With this in mind we can move meetings forward.

Thinking of meetings as vehicles, as the means to an end, clarifies objectives and itineraries. It enables us to get in the drivers seat and focus our attention on the results we want to achieve and the means of achieving them. This requires selecting the appropriate type and structure of meeting, picking a competent meeting leader and facilitator, determining the key participants, and identifying critical steps in order to make the best use of peoples' time and energy. The success of meetings is limited only by our understanding of their purpose and our ability to plan and manage them.

(Adapted from: www.theenglishweb.com/doc/articles/getting-the-most-out-of-an-english-business-meeting.php)

Questions

1) What are the two author's pet peeves?

_____

_____

_____

_____

_____

2) How can we achieve the results that we want in the meeting?

_____

_____

_____

_____

_____

b) Business meetings that matter

Meetings come in all shapes and sizes. There are the everyday office meetings, board meetings, seminars -- all the way up to major conferences. And meetings can now be face-to-face, teleconference, videoconference, or online via the Internet. And when is the last time you heard someone say, "Gee, we need to have more meetings." There are more than enough meetings to go around these days, and for a good reason. Meetings are more important than ever. Modern workplaces are built on teams, sharing of ideas, and effective project coordination.

If communication is the lifeblood of any organization, then meetings are the heart and mind. The place where we communicate our ideas, hash them out, share our passion for better or worse, develop new understandings and new directions. It's where deals can happen or fall apart, where strategies are articulated and debated -- in short -- where we engage with others. That's what it's all about, people meeting with people.

Question

1) What are the types of meetings mentioned in the first paragraph?

_____

_____

_____

_____

c) How to make the most of business meetings

Business meetings range from gatherings of small groups of people to large conferences with hundreds, or even thousands, in attendance. It is those mega meetings that many people find stressful. Here are pointers to help you make the most of business meetings and relieve some of the stress you may feel when you find you have to attend one.

What you should do before you go to a business meeting
• **Meet other attendees in advance:** Get to know as many people as possible before you attend the conference.
• **Look your best:** When you look good, your confidence goes up. Make sure your hair and nails are well groomed.
• **Dress appropriately:** Find out what type of attire is needed.
• **Bring clothes that travel well** or bring an iron.   You don't want your clothes to look rumpled.
• **Pack comfortable shoes:** You may be on your feet for long periods of time.

What you should do at the business meeting

- **Introduce yourself to others:** Making the first move may make you feel less vulnerable.

- **Smile:** Smiling (only when appropriate, of course) helps you look approachable.

- **Psych yourself up:** Remember the qualities others like about you.

- **Get people to talk about themselves:** Everyone likes to do this and it will take the focus off you.

- **Beware of alcohol:** You don't want to become too uninhibited.

What you should do when the business meeting is over

- **Take home something valuable:** This could be an idea you may be able to implement or a new person to add to your network.

- **Keep in touch:** Maintaining contact with those you met at the conference will make the next conference easier.

Question

1) What should you do at the business meeting?

_____

_____

_____

_____

_____

_____

_____

d) Participating effectively in business meetings

A meeting is a gathering of people to present or exchange information, plan joint activities, make decisions, or carry out actions already agreed upon. Almost every group activity or project requires a meeting, or meetings, of some sort. Knowing how to hold efficient and effective meetings can help make projects successful. In a good meeting, participants' ideas are heard, decisions are made through group discussion and with reasonable speed, and activities are focused on desired results. Good meetings help generate enthusiasm for a project, build skills for future projects, and provide participants with techniques that may benefit them in their future careers. As a chairperson, a secretary, or a group member, it is crucial to your meeting's success to know what your role is during a meeting. By knowing your duties, you can effectively assume one of these roles and help to attain success during your meetings.

Question

1 What do good meetings help?

_____

_____

_____

_____

_____

_____

_____

Responsibilities of the chairperson
1) recognize the importance of understanding the role of the chair.
2) recognize the techniques for managing the discussion of issues.
3) manage the discussion of issues, in a business meeting example.
4) match the strategies for managing people to examples.
5) use the strategies to manage participants in a simulated business meeting.
6) recognize the steps for managing time.
7) effectively manage time in a simulated business meeting.

Responsibilities of the secretary
1) recognize the benefits of understanding the responsibilities of the secretary.
2) identify the activities that the secretary can perform prior to a meeting.
3) match the principles for taking minutes to their characteristics.
4) effectively apply the principles for taking minutes for a simulated business meeting.
5) identify the elements required to effectively prepare the minutes of a business meeting for distribution.

Responsibilities of the members
1) recognize the importance of understanding the role of the members.
2) identify strategies to fulfill the members' role to help keep a meeting on track.
3) identify how members should prepare for a business meeting.
4) identify the strategies that will help group members to actively participate in a business meeting.
5) apply effective participation guidelines during a simulated meeting.

Question

1) What are the responsibilities of the chairperson?

_____

_____

_____

_____

_____

_____

_____

_____

_____

_____

_____

e) Leading effective business meetings

Since there are more than 11 million meetings held every day in the United States, there is a good chance that your life is full of meetings. There is a general agreement among business professionals that most meetings are not well run. They often waste your time, drain your energy, seem to have no purpose, and bear few positive results. Are you tired of attending meetings like this? Are you tired of your meetings ending up like this? This course will teach you how to make your meetings more successful by providing the tools and information that are necessary to lead an effective meeting.

f) Making the most of your time during meetings

1) recognize the benefits of understanding how to use time effectively during business meetings.

2) identify techniques for finishing a meeting on time.

3) identify examples of what a leader should say during the phases of a meeting.

4) match types of questions that encourage participation during a meeting to examples of when they should be used.

5) ask appropriate questions to encourage participation during a given meeting.

6) recognize the tips for avoiding groupthink.

i) Tools for effective meeting leaders
1) recognize the benefits of understanding how to use tools for leading a meeting.
2) identify reasons for using icebreakers during a meeting.
3) recognize the importance of rules of order.
4) match types of audiovisual equipment to the circumstances under which they should be used.

j) Leading various types of meetings
1) recognize the benefits of knowing how to lead various types of meetings.
2) identify guidelines for leading a virtual meeting.
3) match decision-making techniques to examples of circumstances under which they should be used.
4) determine the appropriate decision-making technique to use in a given scenario.
5) identify the steps for guiding a group through a problem-solving meeting.
6) apply the steps for guiding a group through a problem-solving meeting, given a scenario.

j) Leading various types of meetings

7) Have everyone write on a piece of paper their answers to these questions: What is your favorite food, animal, TV show, hobby, and color? Sign your name. Don't let anyone else see the answers. The leader then reads the answers to the whole group, and members try to guess whom each set of answers belongs to. Award one point for each right guess. The person with the most points wins a prize.

8) Give each person is given a list of 5 to 10 traits that they must find in common with the people around them. Sample items could be: "Find someone that was born in the same month", "..someone who lives in your state", or "..drives the same model of car". A prize is awarded to the participants with the most in common.

Review questions:

1. What is a meeting? Give some examples.

_____

_____

_____

_____

_____

_____

2. What should you do at the business meeting?

_____

_____

_____

_____

_____

3. What are the responsibilities of a chairman?

_____

_____

_____

_____

_____

4. What are the responsibilities of a secretary?

_____

_____

_____

_____

_____

_____

5. What are the responsibilities of a member?

_____

_____

_____

_____

_____

_____

Task 3: Listening

Instructions: A) Listen to the following meeting discussion, then fill in the missing words you hear in the blanks. Some key vocabulary you are going to hear is given below:

Key Vocabulary

- survey *(noun)*: questionnaire or a detailed critical inspection
  - The company is conducting a <u>survey</u> to find out what new products its customers want.
- leisure *(adjective; also noun)*: time available for ease and relaxation
  - I try to set aside an hour or so every weekend for <u>leisure</u> activities with my children.
- summarize *(verb)*: sum up or give a summary of
  - The president doesn't have the time to read the whole report, so you better <u>summarize</u> it for him.
- break down *(verb)*: to analyze data into different categories; also to stop functioning because of mechanical failure
  - The student population at this school can be <u>broken down</u> into several main groups.
- compile *(verb)*: put together, collect or accumulate
  - I need to <u>compile</u> the data and write the report by Friday.

- cite *(verb)*: to make reference to or mention
  - The president <u>cited</u> several reasons for poor earnings during the latter part of the year.
- target *(verb)*: to aim at or set a goal toward
  - The management has decided to <u>target</u> their new line of laptops at university students.
- appealing *(adjective)*: able to attract interest or draw favorable attention
  - Changing the decor of the restaurant will create a more <u>appealing</u> atmosphere for older customers.
- slogan *(noun)*: a favorite saying or motto
  - We need to come up with a new <u>slogan</u> that will better represent our product.
- iron out *(verb)*: straighten out, settle, or resolve
  - I prefer not to proceed with the plan until we <u>iron out</u> some of the details.

Now listen...

Somchai: Saman, could you (1)_____ the results of the survey on leisure sporting activities again? We need to plan out our (2)_____ for this Friday's business meeting.

Saman: Sure, Somchai. I've summarized the results in the handout, broken down by (3)_____ age groups and sporting activities. The survey was administered to 550 men and women between the ages of 18 and 55 years old, and the results have been compiled in the following age groups: 18 to 26, 27 to 35, 36 to 45, and 46 to 55. According to the results, the most (4)_____ group involved in sporting

activities are those between 18 and 26 years old, followed by those 36 to 45
years old.

Somchai: Okay.

Saman: As far as particular sports are concerned, people in these two groups (5)_____
jogging as their favorite recreational sport followed by skiing, tennis, swimming, and cycling.

Somchai: And what about these groups broken down by (6)_____?

Saman: Oh, Somchai, thanks for bringing that up. Men appear to be slightly more active than women in the 18 to 26 year-old age group, but women seem more active in the other three groups.

Somchai: Hmm. Based on what you have said, I think we should (7)_____ targeting the 18 to 26 year-old age group more in the future. I also feel we should consider expanding our line of athletic shoes, particularly jogging and tennis (8)_____.
We also have to come up with a more appealing slogan aimed at this age group.

Saman: I see what you mean. However, when these results are compared with the survey carried out three years ago, we can see a growing (9)_____
among older consumers--those 14, I mean 46 to 55--who are becoming more conscious and concerned about staying fit. I believe this trend will continue, so we should focus on this group instead.

Somchai: I see your point. Well, let's meet again on Wednesday to iron out more of the (10)_____ of this proposal.

Instructions: B) Listen to the same dialogue and choose the best answer (A, B, or C) for the following questions.

1. What was the main focus of the survey?
- ☐ A. leisure sporting activities
- ☐ B. average age of athletes
- ☐ C. durability of sporting equipment

2. Which group seems to be most active in sports?
- ☐ A. 18-26
- ☐ B. 27-35
- ☐ C. 36-45

3. Which sport was cited as the third most popular?
- ☐ A. jogging
- ☐ B. tennis
- ☐ C. cycling

4. What is NOT one of Gary's marketing strategies?

☐ A. target the 18 to 26 year-old age

☐ B. sell tennis rackets

☐ C. carry more athletic shoes

5. Why does Sam want to target the 46-55 age group?

☐ A. They have more buying power.

☐ B. They are very health conscious.

☐ C. They tend to enjoy sports more.

UNIT 3

BUSINESS MEETINGS IN ACTION

OBJECTIVES

Upon the completion of this unit, students should have been able to:

1) Call a meeting
2) Open the meeting
3) Follow the agenda
4) Take the minutes
5) Close the meeting
6) Understand new vocabulary

Task 1: Warm-up activity.

Instructions: Read through the text and study the following vocabulary.

Whether you are holding a meeting or attending a meeting, it is important that you understand key English phrases and expressions related to meetings. A successful meeting has no surprises. With proper preparation and careful organization, a meeting can run smoothly. The most typical complaint about meetings is that they run too long. Meetings that run longer than necessary can be very costly to a company or business. As the famous business expression says: *Time is money.* Setting goals and time limits, keeping to the agenda, and knowing how to refocus, are key components of an effective meeting. This may sound simple in your own native language, but it is a little trickier when you or the participants do not speak fluent English. This unit will help you hold or attend a meeting with success.

1) Vocabulary

Word *Part of speech*	Meaning	Example Sentence
absent *adj*	not present	The vice president is **absent** due to unforeseen circumstances.
accomplish *verb*	succeed in doing	We have a lot to **accomplish** today, so let's begin.
address *verb*	deal with; speak on	I hope we do not have to **address** this matter again in the future.

Word *Part of speech*	Meaning	Example Sentence
adjourn *verb*	close a meeting	If there are no further comments, we will **adjourn** the meeting here.
agenda *noun*	list of objectives to cover in a meeting	Please forward the **agenda** to anyone who is speaking at the meeting.
A.G.M. *noun(abbr.)*	Annual (yearly) General Meeting	We always vote for a new chairperson at the **A.G.M.**
allocate *verb*	assign roles/tasks to certain people	I forgot to **allocate** someone to bring refreshments.
A.O.B. *noun(abbr.)*	Any Other Business (unspecified item on agenda)	The last item on the agenda is **A.O.B.**
apologies *noun*	item on agenda announcing people who are absent; apologies for absence	Everyone is present today, so we can skip the **apologies**.
ballot *noun*	a type of vote, usually in writing and usually secret	Please fold your **ballot** in half before you place it in the box.
board of directors *noun*	group of elected members of an organization/company who meet to make decisions	The **board of directors** meets once a month to discuss the budget.
boardroom *noun*	a large meeting room, often has one long table and many chairs	The **boardroom** is reserved for a managers' meeting, so we'll have to meet in the lounge.
brainstorm *verb*	thinking to gather ideas	Let's take a few minutes and **brainstorm** some ways that we can cut costs.
casting vote *noun*	deciding vote (usually by the chairman) when the votes are otherwise equal	The role of treasurer was decided based on the chairman's **casting vote**.

Word *Part of speech*	Meaning	Example Sentence
chairperson/c hair *noun*	the person who leads or presides at a meeting	As **chair**, it is my pleasure to introduce to you, Mr. Allan Davis.
clarification/v erification *noun*	explanation/proof that something is true/understood	Before we address this matter, I'll need some **clarification** as to who was involved.
closing remarks *noun*	last thoughts spoken in a meeting (i.e. reminders, thank yours)	I just have a few **closing remarks** and then you will all be free to go.
collaborate *verb*	work together as a pair/group	The board fell apart because the members had difficulty **collaborating**.
commence *verb*	begin	We will **commence** as soon as the last person signs the attendance sheet.
comment *verb or noun*	express one's opinions or thoughts	If you have a **comment**, please raise your hand rather than speak out.
conference *noun*	formal meeting for discussion, esp. a regular one held by an organization	Before the **conference** there will be a private meeting for board members only.
conference call *noun*	telephone meeting between three or more people in different locations	Please make sure I have no interruptions while I'm on the **conference call**.
confidential *adjective*	private; not to be shared	Any financial information shared during this meeting should be kept **confidential**.
consensus *noun*	general agreement	If we cannot come to a **consensus** by the end of the meeting we will put it to a vote.
deadline *noun*	due date for completion	The **deadline** for buying tickets to the conference is May 25th.
designate *verb*	assign	If no one volunteers to take the minutes I will be forced to **designate** someone.

Word *Part of speech*	Meaning	Example Sentence
formality *noun*	a procedure (often unnecessary) that has to be followed due to a rule	Everyone knows who is going to be the next vice president, so this vote is really just a **formality**.
grievance *noun*	complaint	The first item on the agenda relates to a **grievance** reported by the interns.
guest speaker *noun*	person who joins the group in order to share information or deliver a speech	I am delighted to welcome our **guest speaker** Holly, who is going to be offering some sales pitch tips.
implement *verb*	make something happen; follow through	It's not a question of whether or not we're going to use this idea, it's whether or not we know how to **implement** it.
mandatory *adjective*	required	It is **mandatory** that all supervisors attend Friday's meeting.
minutes *noun*	a written record of everything said at a meeting	Before we begin with today's meeting, let's quickly review the **minutes** from last month.
motion *noun*	a suggestion put to a vote	The **motion** to extend store hours has been passed.
objectives *noun*	goals to accomplish	I'm pleased that we were able to cover all of the **objectives** today within the designated time.
opening remarks *noun*	chairperson or leader's first words at a meeting (i.e. welcome, introductions)	As I mentioned in my **opening remarks,** we have to clear this room before the end of the hour.
overhead projector *noun*	machine with a special light that projects a document onto a screen or wall so that all can see	I'm going to put a pie chart on the **overhead projector** so that everyone can visualize how our profits have declined.
participant *noun*	person who attends and joins in on an event	Can I have a show of hands of all of those who were **participants** in last year's conference?

Word *Part of speech*	Meaning	Example Sentence
proxy vote *noun*	a vote cast by one person for or in place of another	There must have been one **proxy vote** because I count twelve ballots but only eleven attendees.
punctual *adjective*	on time (not late)	Firstly, I want to thank you all for being **punctual** despite this early meeting.
recommend *verb*	suggest	I **recommend** that you sit closer to the front if you have trouble hearing.
show of hands *noun*	raised hands to express an opinion in a vote	From the **show of hands** it appears that everyone is in favor of taking a short break.
strategy *noun*	plan to make something work	We need to come up with a **strategy** that will allow us to have meetings less frequently.
unanimous *adj*	in complete agreement; united in opinion	The vote was **unanimous** to cut work hours on Fridays.
vote *verb or noun*	to express (the expression of) an opinion in a group by voice or hand etc	We need to **vote** for a new vice chairperson now that Jerry is retiring.
wrap up *verb*	finish	Let's **wrap up** here so that we can get back to our desks.

Task 2: Calling a meeting

Instructions: Study the process of how to call a meeting, and answer the questions that follow.

1. Calling a Meeting

There are a number of ways that you may call or be called to a meeting. Some meetings are announced by e-mail, and others are posted on bulletin boards. If a meeting is announced at the end of another meeting, it is important to issue a reminder. A reminder can also come in the form of an e-mail or notice. Verbal announcements or reminders should always be backed up by documented ones. The date, location, time, length, and purpose of the meeting should be included. It is also important to indicate exactly who is expected to attend, and who is not. If you are planning on allocating someone to take on a certain role, make personal contact with that person to inform them of his or her duty.

1.1 Sample E-mail:

To: jandara@yahoo.com
cc: prasit@yahoo.com; prasarn@yahoo.com; pongpon@yahoo.com;naree@yahoo.com
From:dhirawit99@yahoo.com
Subject: Meeting
Hi Everyone,
We will be having a meeting next Friday from 2:00 PM-4:00 PM in Room 3.
All supervisors are expected to attend. The purpose of the meeting is to
discuss the upcoming tourist season. As you probably have heard, this
could be our busiest season to date. There are already twenty bus tours
booked from Japan, and fifteen walking tours booked from North America.
We are also expecting Korean and Australian tours in late summer. Please
make arrangements to have other staff members cover your duties during
the meeting.
Thank you,
Dhirawit

1.2 Sample Notice:

MEETING
LOCATION: Room 3, School of English
DATE: Friday, May 5th, 2007
TIME: 2:00 PM-4:00 P.M.
FOR: Instructors only
SUBJECT: Final Exam
ATTENDANCE IS MANDATORY

1.3 Writing an agenda

In order to keep the meeting on task and within the set amount of time, it is important to have an agenda. The agenda should indicate the order of items and an estimated amount of time for each item. If more than one person is going to speak during the meeting, the agenda should indicate whose turn it is to "have the floor". In some cases, it may be useful to forward the agenda to attendees before the meeting. People will be more likely to participate in a meeting, by asking questions or offering feedback, if they know what is going to be covered.

Sample agenda:

1 Welcome, Introduction: Tum (5 minutes)

2 Minutes from previous meeting: Jandara (10 minutes)

3 Japan Tours: Dhirawit (15 minutes)

4 N.A. Tours: Prasit (15 minutes)

5 Korean Tours: Prasarn (15 minutes)

6 Australian Tours: Pongpon (if time allows 10 minutes)

7 Feedback from last year: Everyone (15 minutes)

8 Vote on staff picnic: Everyone (15 minutes)

9 Questions/Closing remarks/Reminders: Everyone (5 minutes)

1.4 Allocating roles

The person in charge of calling and holding a meeting may decide to allocate certain roles to other staff members. Someone may be called upon to take the minutes, someone may be asked to do roll call, and someone may be asked to speak on a certain subject. This should be done either in person, or in an e-mail.

Sample personal request: Practice it in pairs

Dhirawit: Hi Jandara, did you get my e-mail about next week's meeting?

Jandara: Yes, I'll be there.

Dhirawit: Great. I'd like to put you in charge of reviewing the minutes from last meeting for us.

Jandara: Sure, I can do that. I think there is a copy of the minutes in my file.

Dhirawit: Thanks, you'll have ten minutes to remind us of what we discussed last meeting. This will be good for Sopha to hear. Sopha will be our new private tours coordinator.

Sample E-mail:

To: jandara@yahoo.com
From:dhirawit99@yahoo.com
Subject: Minutes
Hi Jandara,
I just wanted to make sure that you would be available to review last month's minutes and present them at Friday's meeting. We have a new staff member joining us, so I'd like to give her a chance to see where things have been going since the last meeting. If you have any concerns about this, let me know.
Thanks,
Dhirawit

Questions

1. There are a number of ways that you may call or be called to a meeting. Give some examples.

_____

_____

_____

_____

_____

_____

2. What does it mean by, "allocating roles"?

_____

_____

_____

_____

_____

_____

3. Why is it important to have an agenda, and what should the agenda indicate?

_____

_____

_____

_____

_____

_____

Task 3: Opening a meeting

Instructions: Individually, in pairs, or in groups, practice the following sample dialogues of a small talk, welcome, and introductions, and then answer the questions that follow.

1 Small talk

Whether you are holding the meeting or attending the meeting it is polite to make small talk while you wait for the meeting to start. You should discuss things unrelated to the meeting, such as weather, family, or weekend plans.

Sample dialogue: Practice in pairs

Dhirawit:	Hi Thomas. How are you?
Thomas:	Great thanks, and you?
Dhirawit:	Well, I'm good now that the warm weather has finally arrived.
Thomas:	I know what you mean. I thought winter was never going to end.
Dhirawit:	Have you dusted off your golf clubs yet?
Thomas:	Funny you should ask. I'm heading out with my brother-in-law for the first round of the year on Saturday.

2 Welcome: Practice these sentences individually

Once everyone has arrived, the chairperson, or whoever is in charge of the meeting should formally welcome everyone to the meeting and thank the attendees for coming.

✓ Well, since everyone is here, we should get started.
✓ Hello, everyone. Thank you for coming today.
✓ I think we'll begin now. First I'd like to welcome you all.
✓ Thank you all for coming at such short notice.
✓ I really appreciate you all for attending today.
✓ We have a lot to cover today, so we really should begin.

Sample welcome: Practice it individually

Dhirawit: I think we'll begin now. First I'd like to welcome you all and thank everyone for coming especially at such short notice. I know you are all very busy and it's difficult to take time away from your daily tasks for meetings.

---

3 Introductions: Practice these sentences individually

If anyone at the meeting is new to the group, or if there is a guest speaker, this is the time when introductions should be made. The person in charge of the meeting can introduce the new person, or ask the person to introduce him or herself.

✓ I'd like to take a moment to introduce our new tour coordinator.
✓ I know most of you, but there are a few unfamiliar faces.
✓ Saowapa, would you like to stand up and introduce yourself?
✓ Hi everyone. I'm Chalita. I'll be acting as Dr. Dhirawit's assistant while Naree is away on maternity leave.

4 Roll call/Apologies: Practice these sentences individually

If the meeting is a small group, it is probably unnecessary to take attendance out loud. The person who is taking the minutes will know everyone personally and can indicate who is present and who is absent. In a larger meeting, it may be necessary to send around an attendance sheet or call out names. If an important figure is absent, it may be necessary for the chairperson to apologize for his or her absence and offer a brief explanation for it.

✓ It looks like everyone is here today.
✓ If you notice anyone missing, please let Jane know so that she can make a note of it.
✓ Unfortunately, Komkrit cannot join us today. He has been called away on business
✓ Manop will be standing in to take the minutes today, as Wanwisa is home with the flu.

5 Objectives

Some people who hold meetings prefer to pass around copies of the agenda, and others will post a large copy on a wall, or use an overhead projector. No matter which format is used, attendees should be able to follow the agenda as the meeting progresses. Before beginning the first main item on the agenda, the speaker should provide a brief verbal outline the objectives.

Sample introduction to the agenda: Practice it individually

Dhirawit: As you can all see here on the agenda we will be mainly talking about the upcoming tourist season. First we'll discuss the groups that will be coming in from Japan. After that we'll discuss the North American Tours, followed by the Korean tours. If time allows we will also discuss the Australian tours which are booked for early September. Next, I'm going to request some feedback from all of you concerning last year's tours and where you think we can improve. And finally, we'll be voting on where and when to have this year's staff picnic.

Questions:

1. Is it polite to make small talk while you wait for the meeting to start? And what should you discuss?

_____
_____
_____
_____
_____
_____

2. Who should formally welcome everyone to the meeting and thank the attendees for coming?

_____

_____

_____

_____

_____

_____

3. If anyone at the meeting is new to the group, who can introduce the new person, or ask the person to introduce him or herself?

_____

_____

_____

_____

_____

_____

Task 4: Following the agenda

Instructions: Study the process of how to follow the agenda, and answer the questions that follow.

1 Taking the minutes

Anyone, including you, may be assigned to take the minutes at a meeting. Often someone who is not participating in the meeting will be called upon to be the minute-taker. Before a meeting the minute-taker should review the following:

• The minutes from previous meeting
• All of the names of the attendees (if possible)
• The items on the agenda

It also helps to create an outline before going to the meeting. An outline should include the following:

• A title for the meeting
• The location of the meeting
• A blank spot to write the time the meeting started and ended
• The name of the chairperson
• A list of attendees that can be checked off(or a blank list for attendees to sign)
• A blank spot for any attendees who arrive late or leave early

Sample minutes outline:

Instructors' Meeting
Friday, May 5th, 2007
Room 3, School of English
Start: _____ Finish: _____
Chair: Payom K.
Attendees:
1._____
2._____
3._____
4._____
5._____
Late to arrive:_____
Early to depart:_____

The minute-taker can use a pen and paper or a laptop computer and does not need to include every word that is spoken. It is necessary to include important points and any votes and results. Indicating who said what is also necessary, which is why the minute-taker should make sure to know the names of the attendees. If you cannot remember someone's name, take a brief note of their seating position and find out their name after the meeting. A minute-taker should type out the minutes immediately after the meeting so that nothing is forgotten.

2 Watching the time

One of the most difficult things about holding an effective meeting is staying within the time limits. A good agenda will outline how long each item should take. A good chairperson will do his or her best to stay within the limits. Here are some expressions that can be used to keep the meeting flowing at the appropriate pace.

• I think we've spent enough time on this topic.
• We're running short on time, so let's move on.
• We're running behind schedule, so we'll have to skip the next item.
• We only have fifteen minutes remaining and there's a lot left to cover.
• If we don't move on, we'll run right into lunch.
• We've spent too long on this issue, so we'll leave it for now.
• We'll have to come back to this at a later time.
• We could spend all day discussing this, but we have to get to the next item.

3 Regaining focus

It is easy to get off topic when you get a number of people in the same room. It is the chairperson's responsibility to keep the discussion focused. Here are some expressions to keep the meeting centered on the items as they appear on the agenda.

• Let's stick to the task at hand, shall we?
• I think we're steering off topic a bit with this.
• I'm afraid we've strayed from the matter at hand.
• You can discuss this among yourselves at another time.
• We've lost sight of the point here.
• This matter is not on today's agenda.
• Let's save this for another meeting.
• Getting back to item number 5...
• Now where were we? Oh yes, let's vote.

4 Voting

When issues cannot be resolved or decisions cannot be easily made, they are often put to a vote. Most votes occur during meetings. Votes can be *open*, where people raise their hands in favor or in opposition of the issue. In an open vote, the results are evident immediately. Other votes, such as who should be elected to take on a certain role, are private or *closed*. During private votes, attendees fill out ballots and place them in a box to be counted. The results may not be counted until after the meeting. Here are some specific expressions used during open voting:

• All in favor? (Those who agree raise their hands or say "Aye".)
• All opposed?
• Motion to hire more tour guides, moved by Thomas. (Suggestions or ideas that are put to a vote are called *motions*. When a person makes a suggestion, the term to use both during the meeting and in the minutes is *moved*.)
• Motion to hire more tour guides seconded by Nolan. (When another person agrees with the motion, it is *seconded*.)

When a motion is voted and agreed upon it is *carried*. When it is voted and disagreed upon it is *failed*. Most often votes are put to a majority. If there is a tie vote, the chairperson will often cast the deciding vote.

Sample voting session:

Prasit: Okay, now that we've covered most of the business, it's time to vote on the staff picnic. Jane and I have come up with two different ideas. I'll give Jane the floor now, and she'll outline these two options. After that we'll vote. I don't think there is any reason to have a private vote, so I'll just ask to see a show of hands. Jane, would you do the honors?

Jane: Thanks Prasit. Okay, so, as you all probably assumed, we are going to wait until most of the tours have passed through before we have the staff picnic. That way most of you should be able to attend. So we've chosen the last Sunday of September. I hope that works out for all of you. Now, the first option is to have a BBQ at Samila Beach, Songkhla. We would do this on the last Sunday of September. The second option is to have a potluck dinner/pool party in Prasit's backyard. The only problem with this is if it rains, there isn't much in the way of shelter there. I don't think Prasit and his wife will want all of us dashing inside in a thunderstorm.

Prasit: Well, if we had to we could probably squeeze everyone in the basement. Anyhow, those are the options, so let's put it to a vote. All in favor of option number one? Raise your hands please...okay, one vote. And, all in favor of option number two? That's four. Okay, so it looks like a pool party at my house.

Jane: Great. I'll put up a sign up sheet and everyone can write down what they plan to bring.

5 Comments and feedback: Practice each of them individually.

During the meeting, participants will comment, provide feedback, or ask questions. Here are some ways to do so politely:

✓ If I could just come in here...

✓ I'm afraid I'd have to disagree about that.

✓ Could I just say one thing?

✓ I'm really glad you brought that up.

✓ I couldn't agree with you more. (I agree)

✓ Jandara, could you please speak up. We can't hear you at the back.

✓ If I could have the floor (chance to speak) for a moment..

✓ We don't seem to be getting anywhere with this.

✓ Perhaps we should come back to this at another time?

Questions:

1. Who will be called upon to be the minute-taker?

_____

_____

_____

_____

_____

_____

2. What should an outline include?

_____

_____

_____

_____

_____

_____

3. When should a minute-taker type out the minutes? Why?

_____

_____

_____

_____

_____

_____

Task 5: Closing a meeting

Instructions: Study the process of how to close a meeting, and answer the questions that follow.

1 Wrapping up: Practice these sentences individually.

There are different reasons why a meeting comes to an end. Time may run out, or all of the items in the agenda may be checked off. Some meetings will end earlier than expected and others will run late. The odd time, a meeting may be cut short due to an unexpected problem or circumstance. Here are a variety of ways to adjourn a meeting:

• It looks like we've run out of time, so I guess we'll finish here.
• I think we've covered everything on the list.
• I guess that will be all for today.
• Well, look at that...we've finished ahead of schedule for once.
• If no one has anything else to add, then I think we'll wrap this up.
• I'm afraid we're going to have to cut this meeting short. I've just been informed of a problem that needs my immediate attention.

2 Reminders: Practice these sentences individually.

There is almost always one last thing to say, even after the closing remarks. A chairperson might close the meeting and then make a last-minute reminder. Instructions for tidying up the room may also be mentioned.

- Oh, before you leave, please make sure to sign the attendance sheet.

- I almost forgot to mention that we're planning a staff banquet next month.

- Don't forget to put your ballot in the box on your way out.

- If I didn't already say this, please remember to introduce yourself to the new trainees.

- Could I have your attention again? I neglected to mention that anyone who wants to take home some of this leftover food is welcome to.

- If you could all return your chair to Room 7 that would be appreciated.

- Please take all of your papers with you and throw out any garbage on your way out.

3 Thank you and congratulations: Practice these sentences individually.

The end of the meeting is also the time to thank anyone who has not been thanked at the beginning of the meeting, or anyone who deserves a second thank you. Congratulations or Good luck can also be offered here to someone who has experienced something new, such as receiving a promotion, getting married, or having a baby.

• Before I let you go let's all give a big thank you (*everyone claps*) to Thomas for baking these delicious cookies.
• Again, I want to thank you all for taking time out of your busy schedules to be here today.
• Most of you probably already know this, but Manop's wife just gave birth to a baby boy.
• As you leave today, don't forget to wish Sopha luck on the weekend. The next time you see her she will be happily married.

4 Follow up: Practice these sentences individually.

In the closing remarks, the chairperson, or participants may want to discuss the date and time for the next meeting, when the minutes will be available, or when a decision should be made by.

This is also the time to give contact information, such as how to send a question by e-mail or who to call regarding a certain issue.

• We'll meet again on the first of next month.
• Next time we meet I'll be sure to have those contacts for you.
• If anyone has any questions about anything we discussed today, feel free to send me an e-mail.
• The minutes from today's meeting will be posted as of tomorrow afternoon.
• I'll send out a group e-mail with the voting results.

Task 6: Study the following complete sample of a business meeting, and practice it in groups.

Introduction

The following dialogue is an example of a typical business meeting. As you can see from the dialogue, a typical business meeting can be divided into five parts:

This example business meeting is followed by the two sections which provide key language and phrases appropriate for typical business meetings.

Introductions

Meeting Chairman: If we are all here, let's get started. First of all, I'd like you to please join me in welcoming Jack Peterson, our Southwest Area Sales Vice President.

Jack: Thank you for having me, I'm looking forward to today's meeting.

Meeting Chairman: I'd also like to introduce Margaret Simmons who recently joined our team.

Margaret: May I also introduce my assistant, Bob Hamp.

Meeting Chairman: Welcome Bob. I'm afraid our national sales director, Anne Trusting, can't be with us today. She is in Kobe at the moment, developing our Far East sales force.

Reviewing Past Business

Meeting Chairman: Let's get started. We're here today to discuss ways of improving sales in rural market areas. First, let's go over the report from the last meeting which was held on June 24th. Right, Tom, over to you.

Tom: Thank you Mark. Let me just summarize the main points of the last meeting. We began the meeting by approving the changes in our sales reporting system discussed on May 30th. After briefly revising the changes that will take place, we moved on to a brainstorming session concerning after sales customer support improvements. You'll find a copy of the main ideas developed and discussed in these sessions in the photocopies in front of you. The meeting was declared closed at 11.30.

Beginning the Meeting

Meeting Chairman: Thank you Tom. So, if there is nothing else we need to discuss, let's move on to today's agenda. Have you all received a copy of today's agenda? If you don't mind, I'd like to skip item 1 and move on to item 2: Sales improvement in rural market areas. Jack has kindly agreed to give us a report on this matter. Jack?

Discussing Items

Jack: Before I begin the report, I'd like to get some ideas from you all. How do you feel about rural sales in your sales districts? I suggest we go round the table first to get all of your input.

John: In my opinion, we have been focusing too much on urban customers and their needs. The way I see things, we need to return to our rural base by developing an advertising campaign to focus on their particular needs.

Alice: I'm afraid I can't agree with you. I think rural customers want to feel as important as our customers living in cities. I suggest we give our rural sales teams more help with advanced customer information reporting.

Donald: Excuse me, I didn't catch that. Could you repeat that, please?

Alice: I just stated that we need to give our rural sales teams better customer information reporting.

John: I don't quite follow you. What exactly do you mean?

Alice: Well, we provide our city sales staff with database information on all of our larger clients. We should be providing the same sort of knowledge on our rural customers to our sales staff there.

Jack: Would you like to add anything, Jennifer?

Jennifer: I must admit I never thought about rural sales that way before. I have to agree with Alice.

Jack: Well, let me begin with this Power Point presentation (Jack presents his report).

Jack: As you can see, we are developing new methods to reach out to our rural customers.

John: I suggest we break up into groups and discuss the ideas we've seen presented.

Finishing the Meeting

Meeting Chairman: Unfortunately, we're running short of time. We'll have to leave that to another time.

Jack: Before we close, let me just summarize the main points:

1. Rural customers need special help to feel more valued.
2. Our sales teams need more accurate information on our customers.
3. A survey will be completed to collect data on spending habits in these areas.
4. The results of this survey will be delivered to our sales teams
5. We are considering specific data mining procedures to help deepen our understanding.

Meeting Chairman: Thank you very much Jack. Right, it looks as though we've covered the main items Is there any other business?

Donald: Can we fix the next meeting, please?

Meeting Chairman: Good idea Donald. How does Friday in two weeks time sound to everyone? Let's meet at the same time, 9 o'clock. Is that OK for everyone? Excellent. I'd like to thank Jack for coming to our meeting today. The meeting is closed.

(Adapted from Kenneth Beare, www.about.com)

Task 7: Review questions

Instructions: Recall what you have just studied, and then answer these questions and do the activities accordingly.

1. What is a small talk?

_____
_____
_____
_____
_____
_____
_____

2. What is an agenda?

_____
_____
_____
_____
_____
_____
_____

3. How can you follow the agenda?

_____
_____
_____
_____
_____

4. How do you close the meeting?

_____
_____
_____
_____
_____
_____
_____
_____

5. Write an e-mail to call a meeting (on a separate paper).

6. Write a script of the meeting on the topic you have chosen, rehearse it, and then play a role.

7. Watch the VDO on a business meeting and learn something from it.

UNIT 4

HOW TO CONDUCT BUSINESS MEETINGS?

OBJECTIVES

Upon the completion of this unit, students should have been able to:

1) decide when the meeting should be held
2) make the meeting a sincere dialogue
3) spice up the meeting
4) get the most out of the meeting

Task 1: Warm-up activity

Instructions: Number all the items you need to conduct a meeting in order of importance (1-10).

_____Personal Organizers

_____Notebook Papers

_____Computer Notebook

_____Transparencies

_____Slide Projectors

_____Overhead Projectors

_____Calculator

_____Flip Charts

_____Pointer

_____Speaker stand or table

_____Microphone

_____Agenda

_____Visual aids

Task 2: Steps of a meeting

Instructions: Rearrange the following steps of a meeting in the most suitable order (in your opinion). Number 1 is done for you.

___1___ Decide whether you really need to call a meeting. Can the issue be resolved by an individual or a conference call?

_____ Assemble visual aids such as charts, handouts or slides.

_____ Start the meeting at the designated time, regardless of whether everyone is present. Avoid taking too much time to summarize for latecomers.

_____ Start off the meeting with straightforward, easily resolved issues before heading into thornier ones.

_____ Allocate a specific amount of time for each issue. Move through issues, allowing for discussion but discouraging digression or repetition. Use a timer to help monitor the time.

_____ Postpone discussion until the end of the meeting if debate on an issue runs overtime. Make sure to cover the other issues on the agenda.

_____ Follow up: Circulate copies of the minutes after the meeting to remind everyone of conclusions and action plans.

_____ Determine who needs to attend. Try keeping the number of attendees small, as large meetings get unwieldy. Suggest that people attend only the parts of the meeting that involves them. This way you can keep the discussion more focused.

_____ Set definite starting and stopping times.

_____ Prepare an agenda. Explain the goal of the meeting; if there are many goals, decide which ones command priority, and make this clear.

_____ Circulate the agenda in advance to allow attendees to prepare.

Task 3: Reading comprehension

Instructions: Read the following passage and answer the questions that follow.

How to conduct successful business meetings?

Every day and week we attend meetings for staff related issues, planning, root cause, production, management review, and for many other business reasons. Some people spend more time in meetings than in performing their regular duties and responsibilities. Which in turn causes many to work overtime (without pay) to catch up on business communications, organize the in-basket, answering and placing routine memos and calls, and producing reports of their activities. An every business person spends a majority of time handling process or support related activities, instead of creating new opportunities for the company. This article will deal with some reasons for having meetings and how get the most out of meetings.

a) When are meetings necessary and when could information be communicate differently?

There are times when meetings are not necessary. If there is a purpose for a meeting, then a meeting should be scheduled. However, before scheduling a meeting, you may want to ask yourself whether this information is better communicated with a memorandum, report, e-mail, video-conference, or taped message instead of arranging for a meeting. Is having a meeting the best way to communicate the information to the intended parties. If so, arrange for the meeting, and ensure that it is structured as a dialogue for optimum team learning.

b) How to structure a dialogue for team learning.

The premise for most meetings should be the furtherance of team learning. Some meetings are not structured for a learning experience. If the purpose of the meeting is for team learning, it can best be experienced through a dialogue. A dialogue is different mode of communication than a discussion or a talk. In a dialogue, because of its synergistic approach participants share a common meaning. This win-win relationship is often called group-think, but it goes beyond this concept. Dialogue means "through common meaning." In dialogue, people then become aware of their own thinking, its collective effect on the whole, which is capable of constant development and change. And the thought emanating from this activity becomes coherent. Three basic conditions necessary for dialogue:

1. all participants must suspend their assumptions, literally to hold them together as if suspended before us;
2. all participants must regard one another as colleagues;
3. there must be a facilitator who holds the context of the dialogue.

These conditions allow a free flow of meaning to circulate the entire group, by the diminishing of resistance to the flow.

Participants *suspend their assumptions* by being aware of their assumptions and holding them up for examinations. Opinions could be subjective, but they cannot be defended or suppressed. The team must be disciplined to allow this free flow of shared meaning. Stereotypes and negative mental models should be abandoned. Participants will listen without forming opinions. Analyze the thought process and the results. Each participant must ensure open-mindedness, without bias or preconceived ideas.

Dialogue can only occur when a group of people *see each other as colleagues* in the mutual quest for deeper insight and clarity of the inquiry. Seeing each other as colleagues and friends makes for a positive, nourishing environment. Every one in the dialogue is equal, and there are no adversarial relationships allowed. People should leave their position at the door, and no hierarchy can be present in the meeting, except, of course for the facilitator. Fear and judgment must be replaced with love, understanding, and appreciation for difference. No opinion is stupid, but should be evaluate in the context of dialogue. Spirit of inquiry would allow participants to explore the thinking behind their views. Views must be substantiated by fact or opinion put on the board for further evaluation.

The *facilitator* should be a good process facilitator capable of helping people maintain the ownership of the process and the outcome. This person is responsible for guiding and influencing the flow of development by looking at all sides of the observation made by a participant.

c) Guidelines we have found that contribute to effective meetings.

Here are a few guidelines that we have found makes meetings effective.

Clearly Communicated and Distributed Agenda - Purpose of the meeting. Once you have determined that a physical meeting is necessary either at a location or via teleconference, you must determine what the purpose of the meeting is, who should attend and put together the agenda, with or without the input from the participants. A meeting location should be confirmed and booked, refreshments and food ordered, participants contacted well ahead of schedule, presenter given enough time to prepare presentation. Solicit input for the structure of the meeting from presenters and others, if necessary. If there is a need for participants to teleconference, a bridge and time should be booked. This agenda should be sent well ahead of schedule (possibly in form of a memorandum) to all participants. A day before the meeting, send a reminder. Bring extra copies of the meeting agenda to the meeting. The agenda should detail:

• Date and starting time and ending time
• Meeting location (map included, if necessary)
• List of participants and presenters.
• Subjects covered so participants can review and bring material to the meeting for discussion.
• Time limit for presentations or topics so speakers are motivated to present their specific points.

Ensure that the meeting is a dialogue and not a discussion (if it is not merely a presentation). Meetings should not be confused with presentations, management update, forums, and other one-way communication activities. To get the most out of meetings, ensure that the meetings are held in a dialogue mode, with other guidelines added for success. If participants of the meeting are not educated in the dialogue

Assign a Scribe. As the meeting coordinator or owner of the meeting and its process, it is necessary that you assign a impartial person to act as a scribe (note taker). Inform this person of what types of notes that you expect him/her to take. Provide this person with a laptop computer or the least an agenda with space for notes.

Assign a Facilitator /Timekeeper. The Facilitator/timekeeper's duties are to control the meeting to ensure that it follows the agenda, guide the dialogue (process), distill fact findings, and control and maintain the Q&A session, and to provide input to ensure that the meeting is successful. A regular sports-time watch can be used to time speakers and the round robin session.

Round Robin Q&A session. A Round Robin Q&A session often follows after a presentation has been made. Each participants is allotted two minutes to speak his/her mind and address questions, concerns or inputs to the presenter. In the first round every participant must speak. In the second and third rounds, participants may defer from offering their input or yield the time to another participant. It is the facilitator's role to guide this process, to ensure that Q&A session is in line with the topic at hand.

Team ommunications. To continue the dialogue and the success of the team learning, certain communications and protocols should be maintained to continue the free flow of shared meaning, and to resolve issues that came up. The issues put on the parking lot that cannot be resolved at the meeting, should be assigned to a particular owner with a timeline for successful completion and delivery to the team. An action register for these particular issues should be discussed and completed by the team.

Last thought on making meetings effective

The dialogue approach to team learning has proved very effective in my experience. It is recommended that you follow this approach in structuring your meetings. The culture, education level, type of activity and many other factors will determine the final structure of your various meetings. Naturally some meetings will take a different form than others. You may add to this structure any aspects that can greatly influence the outcome and accomplishment of your meetings. If you follow these guidelines, your meetings will become more effective.

(Adapted from Lars G. Harrison. www.altika.com/leadership/Meeting.htm)

Questions:

1. What is the purpose of this article?

_____

_____

_____

2.Before scheduling a meeting, what should you do?

_____

_____

_____

_____

3. What is a dialogue? And what are the three basic
   conditions that are necessary for dialogue?

_____

_____

_____

_____

_____

_____

_____

_____

4. What should the agenda detail?

_____

_____

_____

_____

_____

_____

_____

_____

5. Name at least three guidelines that make
   meetings effective.

_____

_____

_____

_____

_____

_____

Task 4: Listening comprehension

Instructions: Listen to the following tips on how to spice up your company meeting and fill in the blanks with the missing words.

1. **Start your meetings, presentations and training sessions with an ice-breaker or warm-up activity.** In a large meeting or a short meeting, the _____ can be a single question that gets people thinking and talking with their neighbor.

2. **Diversify your presentation methods.** If every speaker talks to the audience, in lecture format, even interested heads soon nod. Ask people to talk in _____. Use audio-visual materials such as overheads, Power Point presentations and pictures.

3. **Invite guest speakers** for audience participation and excitement. Your customers have lots to say to your workforce about their needs and quality requirements. One client organization that partners with _____, charitable associations features guest speakers from the organizations that receive their donations.

4. **Encourage questions to get a dialogue going.** Ask people to write down their questions in advance of the meeting and during the meeting. Allow time for questions directed to each speaker as you go. If you can't answer the question immediately and

correctly, tell the people you'll get back with them when you have the correct answer. If questions _____ time, schedule a meeting on the topic.

5. An often-overlooked, but very important, successful meeting tactic is to ask each speaker to **repeat out loud every question** he or she is asked. The person asking the question then knows the speaker understood the question. Other people attending the meeting can hear and know the question, too, not just _____ the question - perhaps incorrectly - from the speaker's response.

6. **Set goals for your periodic meeting.** You can't present every aspect of the company's business at a one hour meeting. So, decide the important, timely issues and spend the meeting time on them. Take into _____ the interests of the majority of the attendees as well. Remember, you have other methods for communicating company information, too.

7. **Formulate the agenda carefully.** Identify the needs and interests of the majority of the participants. Start with good news that will make the attendees feel good. Vary the order of the speakers on the _____ each month.

8. An article in the Wall Street Journal, several years ago, stated that U.S. managers would save _____ percent of the time they waste in meetings if they did two things

correctly. The first was to always have an agenda. The second was **start on time and end on time**.

9. **Organize the physical environment** so people are attentive to the meeting content. No one should sit behind or to the side of your speakers. Make sure there are seats for all _____, and if taking notes is required, a surface to write on, too. Make sure visuals are visible and that people can hear.

10. **Never underestimate the power of food at a meeting.** Food relaxes the atmosphere, helps make people feel comfortable, helps people sustain positive energy levels and builds the _____ of the team.

Task 5: Watching the VDO

Instructions: Watch VCD on how the meeting is conducted and think about the meeting you are going to organize asking yourself:

1) What type of meetings am I going to have?
2) When should the meeting be held?
3) How can I make the meeting interesting?
4) How can I get the most out of the meeting?

UNIT 5

TELECONFERENCE & VIDEOCONFERENCE

OBJECTIVES

Upon the completion of this unit, students should have been able to:

1) understand the concepts of teleconference and videoconference
2) learn about the history and impacts of teleconference and videoconference
3) prepare for future participations in and applications of teleconference and videoconference

Task 1: Warm-up activity

Instructions: Fill in the blanks with the missing words. Use the words given below.

information	*conference*	*support*
live *such as*	*providing*	*interactive*
allow	*locations*	*telecommunications*

a) Teleconference

In telecommunication, **teleconference** is the _____ exchange and mass articulation of _____ among persons and machines remote from one another but linked by a telecommunications system, usually over the phone line.The _____ system may _____the teleconference by _____audio, video, and data services by one or more means, _____ telephone, telegraph, teletype, radio, and television.

b) Videoconference

A **videoconference** (also known as a *videoteleconference*) is a set of _____ telecommunication technologies which _____two or more _____ to interact via two-way video and audio transmissions simultaneously. It has also been called visual collaboration and is a type of groupware. It differs from videophone in that it is designed to serve a _____ rather than individuals.

Task 2: Reading comprehension

Instructions: Read these passages and answer the following questions.

1) History

Video conferencing uses telecommunications of audio and video to bring people at different sites together for a meeting. This can be as simple as a conversation between two people in private offices (point-to-point) or involve several sites (multi-point) with more than one person in large rooms at different sites. Besides the audio and visual transmission of people, video conferencing can be used to share documents, computer-displayed information, and whiteboards.

Simple analog videoconferences could be established as early as the invention of the television. Such videoconferencing systems consisted of two closed-circuit television systems connected via cable. During the first manned space flights, NASA used two radiofrequency (UHF or VHF) links, one in each direction. TV channels routinely use this kind of videoconferencing when reporting from distant locations, for instance. Then mobile links to satellites using special trucks became rather common.

This technique was very expensive, though, and could not be used for more mundane applications, such as telemedicine, distance education, business meetings, and so on, particularly in long-distance applications. Attempts at using normal telephony networks to transmit slow-scan video, such as the first systems developed by AT&T, failed mostly due to the poor picture quality and the lack of efficient video compression techniques. The greater 1 MHz bandwidth and 6 Mbit/s bit rate of Picturephone in the 1970s also did not cause the service to prosper.

It was only in the 1980s that digital telephony transmission networks became possible, such as ISDN, assuring a minimum bit rate (usually 128 kilobits/s) for compressed video and audio transmission. The first dedicated systems, such as those manufactured by pioneering VTC firms, like PictureTel, started to appear in the market as ISDN networks were expanding throughout the world. Video teleconference systems throughout the 1990's rapidly evolved from highly expensive proprietary equipment, software and network requirements to standards based technology that is readily available to the general public at a reasonable cost. Finally, in the 1990s, IP (Internet Protocol) based videoconferencing became possible, and more efficient video compression technologies were developed, permitting desktop, or personal computer (PC)-based videoconferencing. In 1992 CU-SeeMe was developed at Cornell by Tim Dorcey et al., IVS was designed at INRIA, VTC arrived to the masses and free services, web plugins and software, such as NetMeeting, MSN Messenger, Yahoo Messenger, SightSpeed, Skype and others brought cheap, albeit low-quality, VTC.

2) Technology

A modern dual plasma video conferencing system. The Plasma on the left is primarily used to show people during the conference or the user interface when setting up the call. The plasma on the right is used to show data in this case but can be used for displaying a 2nd 'far site' in a multipoint call.

The core technology used in a videoteleconference (VTC) system is digital compression of audio and video streams in real time. The hardware or software that performs compression is called a codec (coder/decoder). Compression rates of up to 1:500 can be achieved. The resulting digital stream of 1's and 0's is subdivided into labelled packets, which are then transmitted through a digital network of some kind (usually ISDN or IP). The use of audio modems in the transmission line allow for the use of POTS, or the Plain Old Telephone System, in some low-speed applications, such as videotelephony, because they convert the digital pulses to/from analog waves in the audio spectrum range.

3) Multipoint videoconferencing

Simultaneous videoconferencing among three or more remote points is possible by means of a Multipoint Control Unit (MCU). This is a bridge that interconnects calls from several sources (in a similar way to the audio conference call). All parties call the MCU unit, or the MCU unit can also call the parties which are going to participate, in sequence. There are MCU bridges for IP and ISDN-based videoconferencing. There are MCUs which are pure software, and others which are a combination of hardware and software. An MCU is characterized according to the number of simultaneous calls it can handle, its ability to conduct transposing of data rates and protocols, and features such as Continuous Presence, in which multiple parties can be seen onscreen at once.

MCUs can be stand-alone hardware devices, or they can be embedded into dedicated VTC units.

Some systems are capable of multipoint conferencing with no MCU, stand-alone, embedded or otherwise. These use a standards-based H.323 technique known as "decentralized multipoint", where each station in a multipoint call exchanges video and audio directly with the other stations with no central "manager" or other bottleneck. The advantages of this technique are that the video and audio will generally be of higher quality because they don't have to be relayed through a central point. Also, users can make ad-hoc multipoint calls without any concern for the availability or control of an MCU. This added convenience and quality comes at the expense of some increased network bandwidth, because every station must transmit to every other station directly.

(Adapted from: www.wikipedia.org)

Questions

1. What does video conferencing use to bring people at different sites together for a meeting?

_____

_____

_____

_____

_____

2. During the first manned space flights, how many kinds of links did NASA use? And what were they?

_____

_____

_____

_____

_____

3. When did IP(Internet Protocol)based videoconferencing become possible?

_____

_____

_____

_____

_____

4. What is the core technology used in a videoteleconference (VTC) system?

_____

_____

_____

_____

_____

5. What is "decentralized multipoint"?

_____

_____

_____

_____

_____

_____

Task 3: Listening

Instructions: Listen to the following two passages and fill in the blanks with the missing words.

1) Impact on the general public

High speed Internet connectivity has become more widely _____ at a reasonable cost and the cost of video capture and display technology has decreased. Consequently personal video teleconference systems based on a webcam, personal computer system, software compression and broadband Internet _____ have become affordable for the general public. Also, the hardware used for this technology has continued to improve in quality, and prices have dropped dramatically. The availability of freeware (often as part of chat programs) has made _____based videoconferencing accessible to many.

For many years, futurists have envisioned a future where telephone conversations will _____ as actual face-to-face encounters with video as well as audio. Sometimes it's just not possible or practical to have a face-to-face meeting with two or more people. Sometimes a telephone conversation or conference call is adequate. Other times, an email exchange is adequate.

Video conferencing adds another possible alternative. Consider video conferencing when:

• a live conversation is needed;

• visual information is an important component of the conversation;

• the parties of the conversation can't physically come to the same location;

or • the expense or time of travel is a consideration.

Deaf and hard of hearing individuals have a particular interest in the development of affordable high-quality videoconferencing as a means of communicating with each other in _____. Unlike Video Relay Service, which is intended to support communication between a caller using sign language and another party using spoken language, videoconferencing can be used between two signers.

2) Impact on education

Videoconferencing provides students with the _____to learn by participating in a 2-way communication platform. Furthermore, teachers and lecturers from all over the world can be brought to classes in remote or otherwise isolated places. Students from diverse communities and backgrounds can come together to learn about one another. Students are able to _____, communicate, analyze and share information and ideas with one another. Through video conferencing students can visit another part of the world to speak with others, visit a zoo, a museum and so on, to learn. These "virtual field trips" can bring opportunities to children, especially those in geographically isolated or the economically disadvantaged. Small schools can use this technology to _____ resources and teach courses (such as foreign languages) which otherwise couldn't be offered.

Here are a few examples of how video conferencing can _____ people around campus:

- faculty member keeps in touch with class while gone for a week at a conference

- guest lecturer brought into a class from another institution

- researcher collaborates with colleagues at other institutions on a regular basis without loss of time due to travel

- faculty member participates in a thesis defense at another institution

- administrators on tight schedules collaborate on a budget preparation from different parts of campus

- faculty committee auditions a scholarship candidate

- researcher answers questions about a grant _____ from an agency or review committee • student interviews with an employer in another city

Task 4: Writing

Instructions: Read these two passages and summarize them in just one paragraph.

1) Impact on medicine and health

Videoconferencing is a very useful technology for telemedicine and telenursing applications, such as diagnosis, consulting, transmission of medical images, etc., in real time. Using VTC, patients may contact nurses and physicians in emergency or routine situations, physicians and other paramedical professionals can discuss cases across large distances. Rural areas can use this technology for diagnostic purposes, thus saving lives and making more efficient use of health care money.

Special peripherals such as microscopes fitted with digital cameras, videoendoscopes, medical ultrasound imaging devices, otoscopes, etc., can be used in conjunction with VTC equipment to transmit data about a patient.

2) Impact on business

Videoconferencing can enable individuals in faraway places to have meetings on short notice. Time and money that used to be spent in traveling can be used to have short meetings. Technology such as VOIP can be used in conjunction with desktop videoconferencing to enable face-to-face business meetings without leaving the desktop, especially for businesses with wide-spread offices. The technology is also used for telecommuting, in which employees work from home.

Telepresence videoconferencing, where participants are able to see each other in reasonable life-like sizes and little delay in video transmissions, has started to make an impact on business meetings. Some good business cases have been built on substitution of international travel with telepresence conferencing.

Videoconferencing is now being introduced to online networking websites, in order to help businesses form profitable relationships quickly and efficiently without leaving their place of work.

(Source: http://www.wikipedia.org)

Your summary:

_____

_____

_____

_____

_____

_____

_____

_____

_____

_____

Task 5: Watch the VDO on how to conduct teleconference & videoconference, and discuss , in groups, about what you have learned from watching the VDO.

UNIT 6

BRAINSTORMING

OBJECTIVES:

Upon the completion of this unit, students should have been able to:

1) understand the concept of brainstorming
2) know the basic rules of brainstorming
3) follow the process of brainstorming
4) use the brainstorming session for business and academic purposes
5) engage in a brainstorming session creatively and effectively

Task 1: Warm-up activity

Instructions: Read these passages and fill in the blanks with the missing words. Use the words given below.

easier	*experience*	*ensure*
coordinate	*purpose*	
participant	*amassing*	*restrictive*
facilitator	*flipcharts*	

How to do traditional brainstorming

First we will explain how to be a _____ in a brainstorming session and then we will give you pointers on how to organize one yourself.

Many people find it _____ to be a participant first, before they run a session, but if you and your colleagues approach learning with a flexible attitude then you should have no problems in running one straight off (but perhaps you should practise on a non-vital topic first to gain _____).

Brainstorming is "a conference technique by which a group attempts to find a solution for a specific problem by _____ all the ideas spontaneously by its members" - Alex Osborn.

How to brainstorm in a medium-sized group

Gather a group of between four and fifteen people together in one room. Have a central person to _____ the proceedings, introduce the purpose of the brainstorming session and to outline the rules. This person should also ensure the rules are followed and should actively encourage the participants. This person is the _____(facilitate=to make easier).

Ideally you will then have a brief warm-up on a totally unrelated and fun topic. This will get your creative juices going and help establish a less _____ mood. You should only start the main topic when the right mood is established.

With the _____ and topic established, everyone in the group shouts out their ideas and they are all written down so that they can be analyzed later. The most common method of recording the ideas is on _____ (large pads of paper) but it's fine to use a blackboard, overhead projector transparencies, a computer or individual pads of paper. A secretary or dedicated writer can be useful and for larger groups you may need two or three to _____ all ideas are captured.

(Adapted from: www.brainstorming.co.uk)

Task 2: Reading comprehension

Instructions: Read the following passages and answer the questions that follow.

Types of brainstorming

a) Group brainstorming

To brainstorm usually means to solve problems by having a group of people discuss them and spontaneously suggest ideas or solutions. A brainstorming session is meant to be very open and non-critical. A "bad" or "silly" idea may lead to an idea that is very helpful, so suggestions are left un-judged at first. It is best to set a rough deadline for this free-for-all part of the session, after which the ideas and solutions are evaluated for whatever usefulness they may have.

Again, it is very important that the ideas are not criticized when first presented. To brainstorm effectively, you can't stifle the creative process. If your group has a difficult time with this aspect of the exercise, you could try having them write their ideas down and submit them anonymously. When nobody knows who suggested which ideas, everyone will feel freer to say what they want.

Unfortunately, you will lose much of the value of the session doing this, because individuals will not be spontaneously feeding off of each others ideas. It may be better than nothing, but try to create that non-critical environment and brainstorm in the open for the best result.

b) Solo brainstorming

To brainstorm by yourself, start by writing down the problem to be solved. Then write it down several more times, restating it each time. "We need to save money for a down payment on a house," may be restated as "We need to buy a house," and "We need to get out of this place." Now just spend thirty minutes writing down all the elements of the problem, and everything that comes to mind. Try several creative problem-solving techniques also, writing down the solutions and ideas that are produced. As with brainstorming in a group, it is important at this point that you don't stifle the creative process by judging your ideas.

When you are done with this part, you should have a mess. Only now should you look at that mess with a critical eye. Pick through for the ideas with the most potential. If you are lucky, the best solution may jump out at you. More often you'll have a few decent possibilities that you have to evaluate further. Brainstorm again if you have to.

Questions:

1.What does brainstorm usually means**?**

_____

_____

_____

_____

_____

2. Is it very important that the ideas are not
   criticized when first presented**?**

_____

_____

_____

_____

3. How do you brainstorm by yourself?

_____

_____

_____

_____

_____

Task 3: Listening

Instructions: Listen to the following passage and then fill in the missing words.

Brainstorming process

Brainstorming with a group of people is a powerful _____. Brainstorming creates new ideas, solves problems, motivates and develops teams. Brainstorming motivates because it involves members of a team in bigger management issues, and it gets a team working together. However_____ is not simply a random activity. Brainstorming needs to be structured and it follows brainstorming rules. The brainstorming process is described below, for which you will need a flip-chart or alternative. This is _____ as Brainstorming needs to involve the team, which means that everyone must be able to see what's happening. Brainstorming places a significant burden on the facilitator to manage the process, people's involvement and sensitivities, and then to _____ the follow up actions. Use Brainstorming well and you will see excellent results in improving the organization, performance, and developing the team.

Brainstorming process

1. Define and _____ the objective.
2. Brainstorm _____ and suggestions having agreed a time limit.
3. Categorize/condense/_____/refine.
4. Assess/analyze effects or _____.
5. Prioritize options/rank list as appropriate.
6. Agree _____ and timescale.
7. Control and _____ follow-up.

Task 4: Writing

Instructions: Read the following 12 brainstorm rules and summarize them in one paragraph.

12 Brainstorm rules

1. Number of members and constitution of group: A minimum of 6 and a maximum of 12 people may participate in a brainstorming session. Less than 6 results in argument, more than 12 means that not everyone gets heard. It is recommended that people from different disciplines (specialists, generalists, the client, and outsiders unconnected to the problem) are included.

2. Duration: The session should last at least 3 hours (or a minimum of 1 hour for smaller projects).

3. Use of time: The facilitator must plan out the 3 hour session, blocking out periods of time to the various areas that have to be covered, and ensuring that the group sticks to the plan.

4. Pre-session requirement: The facilitator must initiate brainstorming 1 to 2 days before the actual session by circulating a memo with:

• Location, time and date of the session
• The subject of the session
• A definition of the end result or product that is wanted
• Any deadlines for end product or idea
• Names of the participants and any special tasks for participants named
• Supporting background information
• Explanation of rules for session

5. Seating arrangement: the group should sit in a circular fashion (around a rectangular 'meetings room' desk is fine) so that everyone can see each other. The facilitator and scribe should sit at one side with the board or flip charts behind them.

6. Facilitator's requirements during session:

- Be able to stand in front of group and communicate objective clearly and interestingly

- Keep the group's energy high and raise it if it fades

- Control dominating participants and encourage shy members to join in too

- Keep group on track and focused on productive objectives

- Put aside personal ideas and views in favor of the group's ideas and input

- Use different techniques to draw ideas from group

- Keep meeting on schedule

- Spot opportunities that come up and are not picked up or developed by group

- Make sure the scribe is capturing all ideas in writing

- Squash all side-conversations with "Just one meeting, please!"

- Act as policeman for the golden rule

7. The Golden Rule of Brainstorming: DEFER JUDGEMENT. All ideas are made welcome. Participants must agree not to laugh at or belittle any idea raised during a brain storm session.

8. Quantity, not quality: as an ancilliary point to the Golden Rule above, aim at quantity of ideas rather than quality. To this end, employ Caesar's military strategy he called *celeritas* - speed! High tempo fast generation of ideas helps keep the internal judge at bay and ensures that the golden rule is obeyed.

9. Encourage active listening: participants will bring greater attention and awareness to the task and will get more information if they commit to actively listening to those who are presenting ideas at any moment.

10. Keep on track: the facilitator must beware of the group veering off into unproductive areas and steer it back to the task at hand. He must also guard against participants making judgments and watch out for "veiled warfare" amongst the more dominant members, steering them back in line with the golden rule.

11. Keep the group energized: if the meeting gets mired and sleepy, take a few minutes to get everyone to stretch and move around. Get some refreshments to keep blood sugar levels stable. Blast out mental cobwebs with some creativity games, some energizing music, a funny video or some jokes. Then re-start the session.

12. Summarize - agree - allocate: as the brainstorm session draws to a close, summarize what has been covered and where you are, obtain the participant's agreement on that and allocate tasks from the list of quality ideas that you have harvested from the session.

Your summary:

_____

_____

_____

_____

_____

_____

_____

_____

Task 5: Solo brainstorming

Instructions: Study this scenario and then write down everything that comes to mind.

The scenario: your business is spending too much on delivery costs. You restate the problem twice, then write down everything that comes to mind. You try a problem-solving technique like the "assume the absurd". This leads you to the idea, "Let's not deliver," which seems crazy since most of your customers are in other states. Then it occurs to you that if you delivered all orders for a city to a central distribution point, instead of to individuals, it would be more efficient. The customer could drive a short distance to pick up their order, with the advantage that they could return the product immediately if they were dissatisfied (no need to pack and ship).You write this idea down and move on. Of course you also write down the obvious, such as "negotiate lower delivery rates," or "find another delivery company." When you are done brainstorming you pick through the ideas and decide on a couple to explore further, before choosing the best solution.

Your ideas:

_____

_____

_____

_____

_____

_____

_____

_____

_____

_____

_____

_____

_____

_____

_____

_____

_____

_____

_____

_____

_____

Task 6: Group brainstorming

Instructions: Study this scenario and do the group brainstorming.

Origin: During the late 1930's and early 1940's, advertising director Alex Osborn developed a technique for generating new product slogans and ad campaign ideas amongst his employees. He would meet with his group around a table, outline the problem and then have them generate ideas willy-nilly. Out of the scores of ideas generated, a few would turn out to be real gems. This idea-generating activity evolved and became known as "**brainstorming**" and it is still being used by top companies and creative individuals all around the world.

Uses: You can use it to generate super ideas for writing, business or any other activity that you are involved in, either through traditional group brainstorming sessions or through solo 'wildcatting' brain storm sessions. Brainstorming is a technique that allows you to generate a large quantity of ideas in a short period of time. It aims to bypass the logical 'censor' mind and access the more creative parts of your brain.

Group brainstorming technique: the session involves a group of 6 to 12 people who are briefed prior to the session on what they will be covering. (Participants are encouraged to generate their own written ideas prior to the session to bring to the meeting.) One of the participants will act as the facilitator to organize and control the session. Someone else will act as a scribe or secretary to takes detailed note of ideas generated. The group should be arranged in a non-threatening seating layout with all participants facing each other, with the scribe and facilitator at one side with flip charts behind them to write down the ideas that are generated. The facilitator steers the session where necessary to keep it focused on profitable topics. The facilitator also encourages everyone to participate, and ensures that no ideas are reacted to negatively. The whole point is to go for QUANTITY of ideas rather than QUALITY. If you focus on quantity, the quality will come.

Your group's brainstorming results:

_____

_____

_____

_____

_____

_____

_____

_____

_____

_____

_____

_____

_____

_____

_____

_____

_____

_____

_____

_____

_____

_____

_____

_____

_____

Task 7: Watch the VDO on a Brainstorming Session and learn something from it.

ANSWER KEYS

UNIT 1: ANSWER KEYS

Task 1: Warm-up activity.

Instructions: Study these top 20 words in business meetings in column A and match them with their meaning in column B by putting the correct letter in front of the words from 1-20.

	A	B
___ t____ 1	A.G.M.	a) a type of vote, usually in writing and usually secret- *secret ballot*
____m___ 2	A.O.B.	b) the person who leads or presides at a meeting; chairperson; chair
___r____ 3	absent	c) in complete agreement; united in opinion
___o____ 4	agenda	d) item on agenda for discussion of what has happened as a result of last meeting
____f___ 5	apologies	e) to express opinion in a group by voice or hand etc - *also n.* - to cast a vote *v.*

	A	B
___a___ 6	ballot	f) item on agenda announcing people who are absent; apologies for absence
___l___ 7	casting vote	g) a written record of everything said at a meeting
___b___ 8	chairman	h) telephone call between three or more people in different locations
___p___ 9	conference	i) general agreement
___h___ 10	conference call	j) a separate point for discussion [as listed on an agenda]
___i___ 11	consensus	k) raised hands to express an opinion in a vote
___q___ 12	decision	l) a deciding vote (usually by the chairman) when the votes are otherwise equal
___j___ 13	item	m) Any Other Business [usually the last item on an agenda]

	A	B
___d___ 14	matters arising	n) a vote cast by one person for or in place of another
___g___ 15	minutes	o) a written program or schedule for a meeting
___n___ 16	proxy vote	p) formal meeting for discussion, esp. a regular one held by an organization
___k___ 17	show of hands	q) a conclusion or resolution to do something to decide *v.*
___c___ 18	unanimous	r) not here; not at the meeting; not present
___s___ 19	videoconference	s) conference of people in different locations linked by satellite, TV,etc.
___e__ 20	vote	t) Annual General Meeting

Original Text

1	A.G.M. /AGM	*abbr.* Annual General Meeting
2	A.O.B./AOB	*abbr.* Any Other Business [usually the last item on an agenda]
3	absent	*adj.* not here; not at the meeting; not present
4	agenda	*n.* a written program or schedule for a meeting
5	apologies	*n.* item on agenda announcing people who are absent; apologies for absence
6	ballot	*n.* a type of vote, usually in writing and usually secret-secret ballot *n.*
7	casting vote	*n.* a deciding vote (usually by the chairman) when the votes are otherwise equal
8	chairman	*n.* the person who leads or presides at a meeting; chairperson; chair
9	conference	*n.* formal meeting for discussion, esp. a regular one held by an organization
10	conference call	*n.* telephone call between three or more people in different locations
11	consensus	*n.* general agreement

12 decision	*n.* a conclusion or resolution to do something - to decide *v.*
13 item	*n.* a separate point for discussion [as listed on an agenda]
14 matters arising	*n.* item on agenda for discussion of what has happened as a result of last meeting
15 minutes	*n.* a written record of everything said at a meeting
16 proxy vote	*n.* a vote cast by one person for or in place of another
17 show of hands	*n.* raised hands to express an opinion in a vote
18 unanimous	*adj.* in complete agreement; united in opinion
19 videoconference	*n.* conference of people in different locations linked by satellite, TV etc
20 vote	*v.* to express opinion in a group by voice or hand etc - *also n.* - to cast a vote *v.*

Source: *Top Twenty Business Vocabulary.*
www.englishclub.com/businessenglish/meetings.htm

Task 3 : Useful phrases and sentences
Questions A:
Instructions: Choose the best answer (a,b,c, or d) for the following questions.

1. Which one is NOT an expression for opening the meeting?
   - a) Good morning
   - b) Good afternoon
   - c) Good evening
   - ✓d) Good night

2. Which one is an expression for welcoming participants?
   - a) I'd like to introduce...
   - ✓b) Please join me in welcoming...
   - c) If we are all here, let's get started.
   - d) I don't think you have met...

3. You can start the principal objectives of the meeting by saying...
   - a) We're here today to...
   - b) Our aim is to...
   - c) I've called this meeting in order to ...
   - ✓d) All of these

4. What do you say when you want to move forward?
   - a) So, if there is nothing else we need to discuss, let's move on to today's agenda.
   - b) Shall we get down to business?
   - c) If there are no further developments, I'd like to move on to today's topic.
   - ✓d) a and c

5. Which is NOT an expression for introducing the agenda?
   - a) Have you all received a copy of the agenda?
   - b) There are three items on the agenda. First,…
   - c) Shall we take the points in this order?
   - ✓d) Would you mind taking notes today?

6. How do you introduce the first item on the agenda?
   - a) Shall we start with…?
   - b) So, the first item on the agenda is…
   - c) Pete, would you like to kick off?
   - ✓d) All of these.

7. Which one is NOT an expression for moving onto the next item?
   - a) Let's move onto the next item.
   - b) The next item on the agenda is…
   - c) Now we come to the question of…
   - ✓d) That's not true.

8. What do you say to summarize the meeting?
- a) Before we close, let me just summarize the main points.
- b) To sum up, ...
- c) Shall I go over the main points?
- ✓d) All of these

9. Which one is an expression for suggesting and agreeing on time, date and place for the next meeting?
- a) Can we fix the next meeting, please?
- b) So, the next meeting will be on... (day), the . . . (date) of.. . (month) at...
- c) What about the following Wednesday? How is that?
- ✓d) All of these

10. What do you say to close the meeting?
- a) The meeting is closed.
- b) I declare the meeting closed.
- c) Can I close the meeting?
- ✓d) a and b

11. Which one is an expression for interrupting?
- ✓a) May I have a word?
- b) I don't think so.
- c) That's great.
- d) I like that.

12. What do you say to give opinions?
　　　　a) I (really) feel that...
　　　　b) In my opinion,...
　　　　c) The way I see things,...
　　✓d) All of these

13. How do you ask for opinions?
　　　　a) Do you (really) think that...?
　　　　b) Can we get your input?
　　　　c) How do you feel about...?
　　✓d) All of these.

14. Which is an expression for agreeing with other opinions?
　　　　a) Exactly!
　　　　b) That's (exactly) the way I feel.
　　　　c) I am sorry.
　　✓d) a and b

15. What do you say to disagree with other opinions?
　　　　a) I agree with you, but...
　　　　b) (I'm afraid) I can't agree.
　　✓c) a and b
　　　　d) None of these

16. Which one is NOT an expression for advising and suggesting?
　　　　a) We should...
　　　　b) Why don't you....
　　　　c) I suggest/recommend that...
　　✓d) I wish I could.

17. What do you say when you want to clarify things?
    a) Have I made that clear?
    b) Do you see what I'm getting at?
    c) Let me put this another way...
    ✓d) All of these
18. Which is an expression to ask for repetition?
    a) I didn't mean that.
    ✓b) I missed that. Could you say it again, please?
    c) Could you come again tomorrow?
    d) What's it like?

19. How do you ask for contributions from other participants?
    a) What do you think about this proposal?
    b) Would you like to add anything, (name of participant)?
    c) Has anyone else got anything to contribute?
    ✓d) All of these.

20. Which one is NOT an expression for keeping the meeting on time?
    a) Well, that seems to be all the time we have today.
    b) I'm afraid we've run out of time.
    ✓c) Absolutely!
    d) Keep to the point, please.

Questions B:

Instructions: Match the language in Column B with their function in Column A.

Meetings – Language

A. Function	B. Language
1. Starting	Many thanks for coming, shall we start?
2. Introducing the subject	We need to discuss..
3. Asking for an opinion	Any views on this? What do you think about..?
4. Agreeing	I agree. I totally agree!
5. Disagreeing	I don't agree
6. Conceding a point	Yes, you are right there.
7. Partially conceding	I can see your point but...
8. Making a proposal	I think we should...
9. Suggesting an alternative	Why don't we...instead?
10. Making an opinion	In my opinion.
11.Asking for participation	Would you mind giving us your views on this, Paula?
12.Presenting alternatives	We can either .. or ..
13. Bringing back the focus of the discussion	We are drifting away from the subject. Can we concentrate on the main points?

A. Function	B. Language
14. Ending	Many thanks for your participation. Its been a productive meeting.

UNIT 2: ANSWER KEYS

Task 1: Warm-up activity.

Instructions: Look up in the dictionary and write out the meanings of the following words.

1. pet peeve(n. AmE): something that you strongly dislike because it always annoys you (BrE.: pet hate)
2. unavoidable(adj.): impossible to prevent
3. dynamic(adj.): full of energy and new ideas, and determined to succeed
4. inspirational(adj.): providing encouragement or new ideas for what you should do
5. destination(n.):the place that someone or something is going to
6. facilitator(n.): someone who helps a group of people discuss things with each other or do something effectively
7. competent(adj.):having enough skill or knowledge to

do something to a satisfactory standard
8. appropriate(adj.):correct or suitable for a particular time, situation, and purpose
9. determine(v.): find out the facts about something, officially decide something
10. strategy(n.): a planned series of actions for achieving something

Task 2: Gap filling

Instructions: Read the following passages about English business meeting and fill in the blanks with the words provided below.

brought involve agenda present language conference
standpoint formal meetings business

Business meetings conducted in English are either formal or informal. The informal variety may involve only a couple of people and take place in the managers, or your own, office. For this type there may not be a set time or agenda. Formal meetings usually involve larger numbers of people and are often held in a conference room. There will be an agenda and minutes (detailed notes) are taken to record what happened in the meeting

An agenda lists out the time and place of the meeting and also the points that will have to be covered. Quite often there is also a section of time allocated to "Any other business" (AOB) where ideas that are not listed on the agenda may be <u>brought</u> up for discussion.

Formal <u>meetings</u> may involve a presentation (sales presentation or otherwise) being given, and details on how to conduct effective presentations are covered elsewhere on this site. It is good to familiarize yourself with the venue, however, should you be asked to <u>present</u> something ad-hoc using the white board or flip chart.

As in all communication, body <u>language</u> is very important. Don't smile too much but again don't look totally bored. Holding a pencil in both hands shows that you are paying attention. Sitting at the corner of a <u>conference</u> table can sometimes give you superiority.

The actual language used in English <u>business</u> meetings is detailed below but is not exclusive. Conceding or partially conceding is a good way to negotiate your point of view into being accepted whereas totally disagreeing, or raising your voice is likely to induce hostility and end up with your <u>standpoint </u>being overturned.

Task 3: Reading comprehension

Review questions:

1) What is a meeting? Give some examples.

A meeting is a gathering of people to present or exchange information, plan joint activities, make decisions, or carry out actions already agreed upon.

Meetings come in all shapes and sizes. There are the everyday office meetings, board meetings, seminars -- all the way up to major conferences

2) What should you do at the business meeting?

• *Introduce yourself to others: Making the first move may make you feel less vulnerable.*
• *Smile: Smiling (only when appropriate, of course) helps you look approachable.*
• *Psych yourself up: Remember the qualities others like about you.*
• *Get people to talk about themselves: Everyone likes to do this and it will take the focus off you.*
• *Beware of alcohol: You don't want to become too uninhibited.*

3) What are the responsibilities of a chairman?

• *recognize the importance of understanding the role of the chair.*
• *recognize the techniques for managing the discussion of issues.*
• *manage the discussion of issues, in a business meeting example.*
• *match the strategies for managing people to examples.*
• *use the strategies to manage participants in a simulated business meeting.*
• *recognize the steps for managing time.*
• *effectively manage time in a simulated business meeting.*

4) What are the responsibilities of a secretary?

• *recognize the benefits of understanding the responsibilities of the secretary.*
• *identify the activities that the secretary can perform prior to a meeting.*
• *match the principles for taking minutes to their characteristics.*
• *effectively apply the principles for taking minutes for a simulated business meeting.*
• *identify the elements required to effectively prepare the minutes of a business meeting for distribution.*

5) What are the responsibilities of a member?

• *recognize the importance of understanding the role of the members.*
• *identify strategies to fulfill the members' role to help keep a meeting on track.*
• *identify how members should prepare for a business meeting.*
• *identify the strategies that will help group members to actively participate in a business meeting.*
• *apply effective participation guidelines during a simulated meeting.*

Task 3: Listening

Instructions: A) Listen to the following meeting discussion, then fill in the missing words you hear in the blanks.

Listening Script

Somchai: Saman, could you *review* the results of the survey on leisure sporting activities again? We need to plan out our *proposal* for this Friday's business meeting.

Saman: Sure, Somchai. I've summarized the results in the handout, broken down by *consumer* age groups and sporting activities. The survey was administered to 550 men and women between the ages of 18 and 55 years old, and the results have been compiled in the following age groups: 18 to 26, 27 to 35, 36 to 45, and 46 to 55. According to the results, the most *active* group involved in sporting activities are those between 18 and 26 years old, followed by those 36 to 45 years old.

Somchai: Okay.

Saman: As far as particular sports are concerned, people in these two groups *cited* jogging as their favorite recreational sport followed by skiing, tennis, swimming, and cycling.

Somchai: And what about these groups broken down by *gender*?

Saman: Oh, Somchai, thanks for bringing that up. Men appear to be slightly more active than women in the 18 to 26 year-old age group, but women seem more active in the other three groups.

Somchai: Hmm. Based on what you have said, I think we should *consider* targeting the 18 to 26 year-old age group more in the future. I also feel we should consider expanding our line of athletic shoes, particularly jogging and tennis *footware*. We also have to come up with a more appealing slogan aimed at this age group.

Saman: I see what you mean. However, when these results are compared with the survey carried out three years ago, we can see a growing *trend* among older consumers--those 14, I mean 46 to 55--who are becoming more conscious and concerned about staying fit. I believe this trend will continue, so we should focus on this group instead.

Somchai: I see your point. Well, let's meet again on Wednesday to <u>iron out</u> more of the *details* of this proposal.

Instructions: B) Listen to the same dialogue and choose the best answer (A, B, or C) for the following questions.

1. What was the main focus of the survey?

◉ A. leisure sporting activities

◻ B. average age of athletes

◻ C. durability of sporting equipment

2. Which group seems to be most active in sports?

◉ A. 18-26

◻ B. 27-35

◻ C. 36-45

3. Which sport was cited as the third most popular?

☐ A. jogging

◉ B. tennis

☐ C. cycling

4. What is NOT one of Sochai's marketing strategies?

☐ A. target the 18 to 26 year-old age

◉ B. sell tennis rackets

☐ C. carry more athletic shoes

5. Why does Saman want to target the 46-55 age group?

☐ A. They have more buying power.

◉ B. They are very health conscious.

☐ C. They tend to enjoy sports more.

UNIT 3: ANSWER KEYS

Task 2: Calling a meeting

Questions

1. There are a number of ways that you may call or be called to a meeting. Give some examples.

Some meetings are announced by e-mail, and others are posted on bulletin boards. If a meeting is announced at the end of another meeting, it is important to issue a reminder.

2. Why is it important to have an agenda, and what should the agenda indicate?

In order to keep the meeting on task and within the set amount of time, it is important to have an agenda. The agenda should indicate the order of items and an estimated amount of time for each item.

3. What does it mean by "allocating roles"?

Someone may be called upon to take the minutes, to do roll call, to speak on a certain subject

Task 3: Opening a meeting

Questions:

1. Is it polite to make small talk while you wait for the meeting to start? And what should you discuss?

Yes, it is. I should discuss about things unrelated to the meeting, such as weather, family, or weekend plans

2. Who should formally welcome everyone to the meeting and thank the attendees for coming?

The chairperson, or whoever is in charge of the meeting

3. If anyone at the meeting is new to the group, who can introduce the new person, or ask the person to introduce him or herself?

The person in charge of the meeting

Task 4: Following the agenda

Questions:

1. Who will be called upon to be the minute-taker?

Often someone who is not participating in the meeting will be called upon to be the minute-taker.

2. What should an outline include?

An outline should include the following:

• *A title for the meeting*
• *The location of the meeting*
• *A blank spot to write the time the meeting started and ended*
• *The name of the chairperson*
• *A list of attendees that can be checked off(or a blank list for attendees to sign)*
• *A blank spot for any attendees who arrive late or leave early*

3. When should a minute-taker type out the minutes? Why?

Immediately after the meeting. So that nothing is forgotten

Task 5: Review questions

Instructions: Recall what you have just studied, and then answer these questions and do the activities accordingly.

1. What is a small talk?

Things unrelated to the meeting, such as weather, family, or weekend plans.

2. What is an agenda?

List of objectives to cover in a meeting

3. How can you follow the agenda?

Staying within the time limits

4. How do you close the meeting?

Here are a variety of ways to adjourn a meeting:

- *It looks like we've run out of time, so I guess we'll finish here.*

- *I think we've covered everything on the list.*

- *I guess that will be all for today.*

- *Well, look at that...we've finished ahead of schedule for once.*

- *If no one has anything else to add, then I think we'll wrap this up.*

UNIT: 4 ANSWER KEYS

Task 1: Warm-up activity. Instructions: Number all the items you need to conduct a meeting in order of importance (1-10). Possible answer.

_____13_____ *Personal Organizers*

_____8_____ *Notebook Papers*

_____4_____ *Computer Notebook*

_____6_____ *Transparencies*

_____7_____ *Slide Projectors*

_____5_____ *Overhead Projectors*

_____12_____ *Calculator*

_____11_____ *Flip Charts*

_____10_____ *Pointer*

_____3_____ *Speaker stand or table*

_____2_____ *Microphone*

_____1_____ *Agenda*
_____9_____ *Visual aids*

Task 2: Steps of a meeting.

Instructions: Rearrange the following steps of a meeting in the most suitable order (in your opinion). Number 1 is done for you.

_____1_____ *Decide whether you really need to call a meeting. Can the issue be resolved by an individual or a conference call?*

_____6_____ *Assemble visual aids such as charts, handouts or slides.*

_____7_____ *Start the meeting at the designated time, regardless of whether everyone is present. Avoid taking too much time to summarize for latecomers.*

_____8_____ *Start off the meeting with straightforward, easily resolved issues before heading into thornier ones.*

_____9_____ *Allocate a specific amount of time for each issue. Move through issues, allowing for discussion but discouraging digression or repetition. Use a timer to help monitor the time.*

_____10_____ *Postpone discussion until the end of the meeting if debate on an issue runs overtime. Make sure to cover the other issues on the agenda.*

_____11_____ *Follow up: Circulate copies of the minutes after the meeting to remind everyone of conclusions and action plans.*

_____2_____ *Determine who needs to attend. Try keeping the number of attendees small, as large meetings get unwieldy. Suggest that people attend only the parts of the meeting that involves them. This way you can keep the discussion more focused.*

_____3_____ *Set definite starting and stopping times.*

_____4_____ *Prepare an agenda. Explain the goal of the meeting; if there are many goals, decide which ones command priority, and make this clear.*

_____5_____ *Circulate the agenda in advance to allow attendees to prepare.*

Task 3: Reading comprehension.

Questions:

1.What is the purpose of this article?

Deal with some reasons for having meetings and how get the most out of meetings.

2.Before scheduling a meeting, what should you do?

You may want to ask yourself whether this information is better communicated with a memorandum, report, e-mail, video-conference, or taped message instead of arranging for a meeting.

3.What is a dialogue? And what are the three basic conditions that are necessary for dialogue?

Dialogue means "through common meaning." Three basic conditions that are necessary for dialogue:

1.	*All participants must suspend their assumptions, literally to hold them together as if suspended before us;*
2.	*All participants must regard one another as colleagues;*
3.	*There must be a facilitator who holds the context of the dialogue.*

4.What should the agenda detail?

The agenda should detail:

•	*Date and starting time and ending time*
•	*Meeting location (map included, if necessary)*

• *List of participants and presenters.*

• *Subjects covered so participants can review and bring material to the meeting for discussion.*

• *Time limit for presentations or topics so speakers are motivated to present their specific points.*

5.Name at least three guidelines that make meetings effective.

1. *Clearly communicated and distributed Agenda - purpose of the meeting*
2. *Ensure that the meeting is a dialogue and not a discussion*
3. *Assign a facilitator /timekeeper*
4. *Assign a scribe*
5. *Team communications*

Task 4: Listening

Instructions: Listen to the following tips on how to spice up your company meeting and fill in the blanks with the missing words.

Listening script

1. Start your meetings, presentations and training sessions with an ice-breaker or warm-up activity. In a large meeting or a short meeting, the icebreaker can be a single question that gets people thinking and talking with their neighbor. As an example, ask a question that causes people to raise their hands. The length of the ice-breaker depends on the length of your meeting, so plan wisely.

2. Diversify your presentation methods. If every speaker talks to the audience, in lecture format, even interested heads soon nod. Ask people to talk in small groups. Use audio-visual materials such as overheads, Power Point presentations and pictures. If you're talking about a new painting process, show your employees before and after parts. Pass around positive customer surveys and comment cards.

3. Invite guest speakers for audience participation and excitement. Your customers have lots to say to your workforce about their needs and quality requirements. One client organization that partners with non-

profit, charitable associations features guest speakers from the organizations that receive their donations. Speakers from organizations your employees support financially are dynamite.

4. Encourage questions to get a dialogue going. Ask people to write down their questions in advance of the meeting and during the meeting. Allow time for questions directed to each speaker as you go. If you can't answer the question immediately and correctly, tell the people you'll get back with them when you have the correct answer. If questions exceed time, schedule a meeting on the topic.

5. An often-overlooked, but very important, successful meeting tactic is to ask each speaker to repeat out loud every question he or she is asked. The person asking the question then knows the speaker understood the question. Other people attending the meeting can hear and know the question, too, not just surmise the question - perhaps incorrectly - from the speaker's response.

6. Set goals for your periodic meeting. You can't present every aspect of the company's business at a one hour meeting. So, decide the important, timely issues and spend the meeting time on them. Take into consideration the interests of the majority of the attendees as well. Remember, you have other methods for communicating company

information, too. It does not have to take place at the meeting.

7. Formulate the agenda carefully. Identify the needs and interests of the majority of the participants. Start with good news that will make the attendees feel good. Vary the order of the speakers on the agenda each month. You don't want people bored by sameness. Distribute important items across the agenda so people don't tune out the end of the meeting, or think the final items are less important.

8. An article in the Wall Street Journal, several years ago, stated that U.S. managers would save eighty percent of the time they waste in meetings if they did two things correctly. The first was to always have an agenda. The second was start on time and end on time. I'll add that you need to allot each speaker the amount of time necessary to cover their topic. Hold them to their time limit - nicely.

9. Organize the physical environment so people are attentive to the meeting content. No one should sit behind or to the side of your speakers. Make sure there are seats for all attendees, and if taking notes is required, a surface to write on, too. Make sure visuals are visible and that people can hear. You may need to use a microphone. You can pass props or samples around the room for viewing.

10. Never underestimate the power of food at a meeting. Food relaxes the atmosphere, helps

make people feel comfortable, helps people sustain positive energy levels and builds the camaraderie of the team. Ensure you meet the diverse needs of your group with the food you serve.

UNIT 5: ANSWER KEYS

Task 1: Warming-up activity

Instructions: Fill in the blanks with the missing words. Use the words given below.

information	*conference*	
support	*live*	*such as*
providing	*interactive*	*allow*
locations	*telecommunications*	

a) Teleconference

In telecommunication, teleconference is the ___ *interactive* ____ exchange and mass articulation of ___*information*_____among persons and machines remote from one another but linked by a telecommunications system, usually over the phone line.

The___*telecommunications*_____system may____*support*_____the teleconference by ___ *providing*_____audio, video, and data services by one or more means, ___*live* _____telephone, telegraph, teletype, radio, and television.

b) Videoconference

A videoconference (also known as a *videoteleconference*) is a set of _ *interactive* ___

---

telecommunication technologies which ___ *allow* ___two or more__ *locations* ___ to interact via two-way video and audio transmissions simultaneously. It has also been called visual collaboration and is a type of groupware. It differs from videophone in that it is designed to serve a __ *conference* ___ rather than individuals.

Task 2: Reading comprehension.

Questions

1. What does video conferencing use to bring people at different sites together for a meeting?

Telecommunications of audio and video

2. During the first manned space flights, how many kinds of links did NASA use? And what were they?

NASA used two radiofrequency: UHF and VHF links, one in each direction.

3. When did IP(Internet Protocol)based videoconferencing become possible?

In the 1990s

4. What is the core technology used in a videoteleconference (VTC) system?

Digital compression of audio and video streams in real time

5. What is "decentralized multipoint"?

A standards-based H.323 technique

Task 3: Listening

Instructions: Listen to the following two passages and fill in the blanks with the missing words.

Listening script

1) Impact on the general public

High speed Internet connectivity has become more widely available at a reasonable cost and the cost of video capture and display technology has decreased. Consequently personal video teleconference systems based on a webcam, personal computer system, software compression and broadband Internet connectivity have become affordable for the general public. Also, the hardware used for this technology has continued to improve in quality, and prices have dropped dramatically. The availability of freeware (often as part of chat programs) has made software based videoconferencing accessible to many.

2) Impact on education

Videoconferencing provides students with the opportunity to learn by participating in a 2-way communication platform. Furthermore, teachers and lecturers from all over the world can be brought to classes in remote or otherwise isolated places.

Students from diverse communities and backgrounds can come together to learn about one another. Students are able to <u>explore</u>, communicate, analyze and share information and ideas with one another. Through video conferencing students can visit another part of the world to speak with others, visit a zoo, a museum and so on, to learn. These "virtual field trips" can bring opportunities to children, especially those in geographically isolated or the economically disadvantaged. Small schools can use this technology to <u>pool </u>resources and teach courses (such as foreign languages) which otherwise couldn't be offered.

(Adapted from: www.wikipedia.org)

UNIT 6: ANSWER KEYS

Task 1: Warm-up activity

Instructions: Read these passages and fill in the blanks with the missing words. Use the words given below.

How to do traditional brainstorming

First we will explain how to be a ___ *participant* _____ in a brainstorming session and then we will give you pointers on how to organize one yourself.

Many people find it _____ *easier* ____ to be a participant first, before they run a session, but if you and your colleagues approach learning with a flexible attitude then you should have no problems in running one straight off (but perhaps you should practise on a non-vital topic first to gain _____ *experience* _____).

Brainstorming is "a conference technique by which a group attempts to find a solution for a specific problem by ____ *amassing* _____ all the ideas spontaneously by its members" - Alex Osborn.

How to brainstorm in a medium-sized group

Gather a group of between four and fifteen people together in one room. Have a central person to _____ *coordinate* _____ the proceedings,

introduce the purpose of the brainstorming session and to outline the rules. This person should also ensure the rules are followed and should actively encourage the participants. This person is the
____*facilitator* _____(facilitate=to make easier).

Ideally you will then have a brief warm-up on a totally unrelated and fun topic. This will get your creative juices going and help establish a less ____ *restrictive* _____ mood. You should only start the main topic when the right mood is established.

With the __ *purpose* __ and topic established, everyone in the group shouts out their ideas and they are all written down so that they can be analyzed later. The most common method of recording the ideas is on ___*flipcharts*
_____ (large pads of paper) but it's fine to use a blackboard, overhead projector transparencies, a computer or individual pads of paper. A secretary or dedicated writer can be useful and for larger groups you may need two or three to _____ *ensure* _____ all ideas are captured.

(Adapted from: www.brainstorming.co.uk)

Task 2: Reading comprehension

Instructions: Read the following passages and answer the questions that follow.

Types of brainstorming

a) Group brainstorming

To brainstorm usually means to solve problems by having a group of people discuss them and spontaneously suggest ideas or solutions. A brainstorming session is meant to be very open and non-critical. A "bad" or "silly" idea may lead to an idea that is very helpful, so suggestions are left un-judged at first. It is best to set a rough deadline for this free-for-all part of the session, after which the ideas and solutions are evaluated for whatever usefulness they may have.

Again, it is very important that the ideas are not criticized when first presented. To brainstorm effectively, you can't stifle the creative process. If your group has a difficult time with this aspect of the exercise, you could try having them write their ideas down and submit them anonymously. When nobody knows who suggested which ideas, everyone will feel freer to say what they want.

Unfortunately, you will lose much of the value of the session doing this, because individuals will not be spontaneously feeding off of each others ideas. It may be better than nothing, but try to create that non-critical environment and brainstorm in the open for the best result.

b) Solo brainstorming

To brainstorm by yourself, start by writing down the problem to be solved. Then write it down several more times, restating it each time. "We need to save money for a down payment on a house," may be restated as "We need to buy a house," and "We need to get out of this place." Now just spend thirty minutes writing down all the elements of the problem, and everything that comes to mind. Try several creative problem-solving techniques also, writing down the solutions and ideas that are produced. As with brainstorming in a group, it is important at this point that you don't stifle the creative process by judging your ideas.

When you are done with this part, you should have a mess. Only now should you look at that mess with a critical eye. Pick through for the ideas with the most potential. If you are lucky, the best solution may jump out at you. More often you'll have a few decent possibilities that you have to evaluate further. Brainstorm again if you have to.

Questions:

1. What does "brainstorm" usually means?

To brainstorm usually means to solve problems by having a group of people discuss them and spontaneously suggest ideas or solutions

2. Is it very important that the ideas are not criticized when first presented?

Yes.

3. How do you brainstorm by yourself?

To brainstorm by yourself, start by writing down the problem to be solved. Then write it down several more times, restating it each time.

Task 3: Listening

Instructions: Listen to the following passage and then fill in the missing words.

Listening script

Instructions: Listen to the following passage and then fill in the missing words.

Brainstorming process

Brainstorming with a group of people is a powerful technique. Brainstorming creates new ideas, solves problems, motivates and develops teams. Brainstorming motivates because it involves members of a team in bigger management issues, and it gets a team working together. However, brainstorming is not simply a random activity. Brainstorming needs to be structured and it follows brainstorming rules. The brainstorming process is described below, for which you will need a flip-chart or alternative. This is crucial as Brainstorming needs to involve the team, which means that everyone must be able to see what's happening. Brainstorming places a significant burden on the facilitator to manage the process, people's involvement and sensitivities, and then to manage the follow up actions. Use Brainstorming well and you will see excellent results in improving the organization, performance, and developing the team.

Brainstorming process

1. Define and agree the objective.
2. Brainstorm ideas and suggestions having agreed a time limit.
3. Categorize/condense/combine/refine.
4. Assess/analyze effects or results.
5. Prioritize options/rank list as appropriate.
6. Agree action and timescale.
7. Control and monitor follow-up.

REFERENCES

Books

Comfort, Jeremy. 2001. Effective Meetings. Oxford: Oxford University Press.

Thomson, Kenneth. 2007. English for Meetings. Oxford: Oxford University Press.

Journal

"How to Use English in Meetings", *Interactive English for Business, vol. 2.* (2 VCDs), 2005. Bangkok: DiD International.

Web sites

http://tesl-en.org/ej28/m1.html

www.abax.co.jp/downloads/extension/BusEnglish_M tgs_extension.pdf.

www.about.com

www.altika.com/leadership/Meeting.htm

www.bbc.co.uk/worldservice/learningenglish/busines s/talkingbusiness/unit2meetings/1agenda.shtm

www.brainstorming.co.uk

www.businessenglishpod.com/FREEsamples/BEP202
QIZ.htm

www.businessballs.com

www.businessmeetings.com

www.englishclub.com/business-
english/meetings.htm

www.esl-lab.com/bs1/bscrt1.htm

www.hkenglish.com/business-meetings.html

www.increasebrainpower.com

www.scribd.com/doc/2740308/English-for-business-
meeting

www.theenglishweb.com/doc/articles/getting-the-
most-out-of-an-english-business-meeting.php

www.wilynut.com